The Early Christian Doctrine of God

The Holy Trinity. English school of the early four-
teenth century. (Courtesy of the National Gallery of
Art, Washington, D.C., Samuel H. Kress Collection)

THE EARLY
CHRISTIAN
DOCTRINE
OF GOD

Robert M. Grant

University Press of Virginia
Charlottesville

Richard Lectures for 1965–66

The University Press of Virginia
First published 1966

Library of Congress
Catalog Card Number: 66–22845
Printed in
the United States of America

FOREWORD

It gives me great pleasure to express my gratitude to the James W. Richard Lecture Committee of the University of Virginia for giving me the opportunity of putting together some of the conclusions I have reached in the course of my studies in the New Testament and early Christian literature. Admittedly there are other approaches to the themes considered here; mine is primarily intended to bring out the continuity between the New Testament and the earlier fathers of the church. What I am trying to show is that early Christian philosophical theology represents a reasonable development out of the New Testament and that although its results can hardly be regarded as final they contain some insights which at least serve as pointers toward the theologies which have arisen in later times.

My thanks are due to many colleagues and students who have discussed these themes with me. Perhaps I should mention especially Professors F. C. Grant, A. D. Nock, and John Knox.

The first lecture was delivered in another version at St. Xavier College, Chicago; St. Michael's College, Winooski, Vermont; the 1965 New Testament Conference, Oxford; the University of Notre Dame; and the Chicago Society of Biblical Research. A portion of the second lecture is based on an address before the 1963 Patristic Conference at Oxford.

Old Testament quotations are often, but not

always, based on the King James Version. Verses 22–31 from Proverbs 8 are from the Revised Standard Version and are quoted by permission of the Division of Christian Education of the National Council of the Churches of Christ in the United States of America. Translations from later Christian and Gnostic literature and from non-Christian writings are usually my own.

R. M. G.

The Divinity School
The University of Chicago

CONTENTS

The Early Christian Doctrine of God

GOD THE FATHER

To A considerable extent the doctrine of God has been neglected by modern theologians (with some notable exceptions), but today they are coming to realize, I believe, that even though they must at present perhaps content themselves with speaking chiefly about the situation, nature, and destiny of man, the fundamental question for the Christian religion is that of the nature of God. Since the Christian religion is based upon traditions reaching back to Jesus and the apostles, and even behind them to the life and thought of Israel, we may perhaps approach the question at least in part in relation to the early Christian doctrine of God. By means of such an approach we may be able to see not only how the theological process

began but also how it went on in its formative period—
which was also one of its most creative eras. We may
even see where some of the perennial problems lie and,
perhaps, how some of them may be solved in relation to
various modes of philosophical-theological thought. It
may even be that the ancient theologians were not as
inadequate as their successors sometimes suppose.

The purpose of this essay is to trace certain aspects of
the doctrine of God the Father in the New Testament
and in early Christian theology and to indicate some of
the bridges between the New Testament and the philosophical language used to interpret it. Here we shall see
how conscious of God's transcendence and of man's
limitations the early Christians were, and how difficult
they found it to make sense of the basic affirmation that
God is love. In a second essay I propose to consider the
development of the early Christian ideas about Christ as
the Son of God, and in a third to examine the doctrine
of the Holy Spirit before turning to the doctrine of the
Trinity. In each case I hope to suggest, with some
measure of plausibility, that (1) the New Testament
ideas find a natural interpretation in early patristic
theology, even though this theology is by no means
final, and that (2) the methods of early Christian
theology make sense in relation to the philosophy of the
time and, indeed, may provide something of a model for
later theologians to imitate. They led neither to irration-
alism nor to the transmutation of the gospel into nothing but philosophy.[1]

[1] I should mention four works which I have found especially
valuable in revising the original lectures. These are the classical
study by G. L. Prestige entitled *God in Patristic Thought* (Lon-

GOD IN THE NEW TESTAMENT

We shall not expect to find philosophical teaching about God in what Jesus said about the Father, whose reign he was proclaiming and, indeed, inaugurating. To a considerable extent Jesus shared the views of his fellow Jews about the God who had revealed himself to Moses and to the prophets. At the burning bush God had said to Moses, "I am the God of Abraham, and the God of Isaac, and the God of Jacob"; he was and is God of the living from one generation to another (Mark 12:26–27). God had spoken a word which was permanently valid for human existence (Mark 10:19; cf. 7:10); indeed, God's purpose from the creation of the world has remained essentially the same (Mark 10:6–9), even though Moses made certain concessions because of the people's hardheartedness (Mark 10:5). This God transcends all human understanding. The sky is his throne and earth is his footstool, even though Jerusalem is "the city of the great King" (Matt. 5:34–35). He makes the sun rise on the evil and the good alike and sends rain on the just and the unjust (Matt. 5:45); he is kind to the ungrateful and the selfish (Luke 6:35). What characterizes him is all-inclusive love. Peacemakers will be called sons of God (Matt. 5:9); men who love their enemies and pray for those

---

don, 1936); the article by W. Pannenberg on "the acceptance of the philosophical idea of God as a dogmatic problem of early Christianity" (*Zeitschrift für Kirchengeschichte* 70 [1959], 1–45); the rectoral address at Zurich by E. Schweizer, *Was heist "Gott"?* (1965); and the important book by R. A. Norris, Jr., entitled *God and World in Early Christian Theology* (New York. 1965).

who persecute them will become sons of the heavenly Father (Matt. 5:45). God forgives those who forgive (Mark 11:25; Matt. 6:12; Luke 11:4), rejoices over repentant sinners (Luke 15:4–32), gives to those who ask him (Luke 11:2–4, 9–13; Matt. 6:9–13, 7:7–11), and knows men's needs even before they ask (Matt. 6:7–8). He is a judge and, indeed, *the* judge; but he is a judge who loves those whom he judges.

The same emphasis on God's loving care for mankind is expressed in the Pauline epistles, for example in a benediction at the end of 2 Corinthians: "the grace of the Lord Jesus Christ and the love of God and the fellowship of the Holy Spirit be with you all." Ordinarily Paul speaks of this love as expressed through the work of Christ, "the Son of God who loved me and gave himself for me" (Gal. 2:20). But for Paul, Christ was "the Son of his love," that is, his beloved Son (Col. 1:13). The chief of the fruits of God's Spirit is love, accompanied by joy and peace (Gal. 5:22).

The proclamation of God's love is especially prominent in the Gospel of John and in the First Epistle. In the Gospel we find that "God so loved the world that he gave his only Son" (3:16); Jesus commands his disciples to love one another as he has loved them (13:34, 15:12, 17). Most of the First Epistle is devoted to God's love for mankind and their love toward him.

The theme of love—"he who does not love does not know God, for God is love" (1 John 4:8)—is one which philosophical theologians were going to treat only with difficulty, as we shall see. From the writings of early Christians after New Testament times we can discover relatively few references to God's love, though a few writers provide exceptions. In general, the themes which were first developed were those related to God's transcendence and his relation to the cosmos. These were themes already under discussion in the philosophical schools, and it was almost inevitable that they should have been discussed by early Christians when the nature of God was being considered.

If we look in the New Testament for "bridges" toward philosophical doctrines of God, we find half a dozen which undoubtedly deserve mention. The oldest of them occurs in the eighth chapter of 1 Corinthians. Paul has begun a discussion of meats sacrificed to idols and turns to a brief discussion of idolatrous polytheism as contrasted with Christian monotheism. "We know," he says, "that there is no God but one." Here he may be echoing the *Shema*, recited in the Jewish synagogue and derived from Deuteronomy 6:4: "Hear, O Israel: The Lord our God is one Lord." After touching upon the "many gods and many lords" of popular belief, he contrasts them with the one God and the one Lord. Here he is partly in agreement with Hellenistic piety, partly not. Maximus of Tyre (*Diss.* 17, 5) states that there is universal consent to the proposition that there is one God, the king of all and father, and that there are many gods, sons of God, co-existing with God. Paul seems to admit the existence, at least contingent, of the many but he insists that

> for us there is
one God the Father,
>> from whom are all things and for whom are we, and
one Lord Jesus Christ,
>> through whom are all things and through whom are we.

This passage is sometimes viewed as credal or semicredal, but for our purposes it is equally important to observe that it is implicitly theological and philosophical. It is theological both because it is an affirmation of faith in God and because it is probably based on another such affirmation in the *Shema*, where we find both "our God" and "one Lord." It is philosophical because its structure is provided by a three-part causal system in which God the Father is the first cause and the last and the Lord Jesus Christ is the instrumental cause—both in creation and in salvation.[2]

Indeed, one might argue that the implication of this passage, taken with another in Romans 11:36, where God is described in terms of all three causes, is that functionally the Lord Jesus Christ can also be described as God. If Paul is really thinking about the *Shema*, the identification of "Lord" with "God" would point in the same direction.[3] Apart from the Christological question, however, it is clear enough that God is being described in language at least related to philosophy.

Another passage suggests that like other Hellenistic Jews Paul had considered the question of God's self-disclosure in natural phenomena. If we look carefully at the structure of the famous verses in Romans 1:19–21, we find that each section can be divided into

[2] See my article in *Journal of Biblical Literature* 83 (1964), 32–40. According to W. G. Kümmel (in H. Lietzmann, *An die Korinther I–II* [Tübingen, 1949], 179), this is an expression of faith; one cannot discuss it but can only agree or disagree. His statement is true as regards the Father and the Lord, not as regards the causal system involved.

[3] Compare also Philippians 2:6–11, where Christ Jesus is "in the form of God," takes on the form of a slave, and finally receives "the name above every name"—"Lord."

two parts. There is what is known or perceived and there is the mode of revelation. First Paul states that the "known" (or "what can be known") of God is evident —for God made it evident. Then he goes on to point out that God's invisible attributes are visible to the mind which contemplates the things he has made "from the creation of the world." These invisible attributes consist of God's "everlasting power and deity." Only if Paul can hold that men possessed this knowledge can he then proceed to say that "though knowing God they did not glorify him or thank him." Indeed, from verse 23 it would appear that they actually possessed some vision of "the glory of the imperishable God."[4]

If we ask precisely what it was that men knew and know of God, the answer is quite clear. They knew his power because of the existence of the things he made. They knew his deity because the power was effected everlastingly. Through the things that God made, men could obtain a mental vision of his glory or presence. Conceivably one could go on to make Paul's statements still more specific and discover by inferences what precisely he had in mind as instances of God's power and his eternity. Indeed, if we were to rely on the sermon excerpts in Acts 14 and 17, we could find almost precisely what we need. In Acts 14 there is mention of God's creating "the heaven and the earth and the sea

[4] With God's imperishability we may contrast (cf. R. Bultmann, *Theologie des Neuen Testaments* [Tübingen, 1948], 225) the "creaturely-transitory" character of the created world; see Romans 8:20–21 ("bondage to perishability"). On the knowledge of God in Romans 1:19 see H. Rosin in *Theologische Zeitschrift* 17 (1961), 161–65; also J. J. O'Rourke in *Catholic Biblical Quarterly* 23 (1961), 301–6, and J. L. McKenzie in *Biblical Research* 9 (1964), 3–13.

and everything in them"; this illustrates his power. There is also mention of his continuing providential concern, especially exemplified in "rains and fruit-bearing seasons" for the benefit of mankind. In Acts 17 we find creation, the seasons, and fixed abodes (perhaps in temperate zones) for mankind. Presumably such points as these, which as Norden and Gaertner have shown are characteristic of popular philosophy,[5] are implied in Romans. But since Paul does not specifically make them in that letter, it is possible that he was thinking more generally.

We should add that when he appeals to "nature" as a norm in 1 Corinthians 11:14 and contrasts the "natural" with what is "contrary to nature" in Romans 1:26–27, he is also saying something about the order of nature as the object of God's creative and providential power and therefore, by inference, something about God himself as Creator and Provider.

In 1 Timothy 1:17—whether by Paul or not—we find two adjectives used of God and they are two which are either expressed or implied in Romans: God is called "imperishable" and "invisible." This language is characteristic of popular philosophy and also of Paul. God is called "invisible" in Colossians 1:15, but this passage is more important for Christology than for the doctrine of God as such.

One more Pauline passage about the knowledge of God deserves attention. This is Galatians 4:8–10, where Paul is criticizing the Galatians for their observance, or possible observance, of "days, months, seasons, and

---

[5] E. Norden, *Agnostos Theos* (Leipzig, 1913); B. Gaertner, *The Areopagus Speech and Natural Revelation* (Uppsala, 1955).

years." If we go through the passage backward, starting with this clear calendrical reference, we next encounter the "weak and impoverished *stoicheia*," which must therefore be astral and planetary and must be spirits because they can be described as weak and impoverished. These in turn must be what he has in mind when he speaks of serving "gods which by nature do not exist" and of not knowing God—that is, the one who by nature *does* exist. Here he may be echoing the famous statement of Antisthenes to the effect that "by law there are many gods, by nature one."[6] We should not claim that Paul had been reading philosophical treatises, but the antithesis of Antisthenes was well known in the Hellenistic world.[7]

From our observation of these Pauline texts we should now proceed to claim that whether or not Paul was directly acquainted with Hellenistic or Hellenistic Jewish philosophy (the possibility should not be excluded), in his letters there exist points of contact with philosophy which later Christians could utilize.

An example of such utilization occurs in the relatively late letter called 2 Peter. Toward the beginning of it we read about Christians becoming "participants in the divine nature" and "escaping from perishability"—a perishability which the author locates "in the world" and "in lust." Quite apart from the question of the

---

[6] Philodemus, *De pietate* (p. 72 Gomperz); indirectly from this treatise to Cicero, *De natura deorum* 1, 32 (cf. H. Diels, *Doxographi Graeci* [Berlin, 1879], 127); directly from Cicero to Minucius Felix, *Octavius* 19, 8 (against W. Jaeger, *The Theology of the Early Greek Philosophers* [Oxford, 1947], 193, n. 9).

[7] See Jaeger, *op. cit.*, 193, n. 10. It does not occur in early Greek Christian writings, however.

deification of Christians, upon which later Greek writers often insisted, it is clear that for this author the essence of the divine nature lies in its imperishability; and this is a thought quite congenial to philosophers in his time.[8]

We should not suppose that such teaching about God was restricted to New Testament writers who were either certainly or possibly in touch with Hellenistic thought. Both Mark (10:18) and Luke (18:19) relate that Jesus said, "No one is good but one, God" (Matt. 19:17 modifies this to read, "One is the good"), thus implying the perfect (Matt. 5:48) goodness of God. In James 1:17 we read that "every good gift and every perfect donation is from above, coming down from the Father of lights, with whom there is no variation or shadow produced by turning." To be sure, James is influenced by Hellenistic rhetoric, but his thought is basically close to Palestinian Judaism. The idea that God is immutable is clearly expressed in Malachi 3:6: "I am the Lord your God and I do not change."[9] Indeed, Plutarch specifically states that Jews and Syrians share the universal notion that God is not perishable and does not come into existence.[10]

It should also be pointed out that in Pauline thought the eternal, imperishable, creative, and living true God is contrasted with temporal, perishable, ineffective, and

---

[8] The statement in 2 Peter is thus more philosophical than that of Josephus (*Contra Apionem* 1, 232), who says that an Egyptian sage "seems to have shared in the divine nature as regards wisdom and foreknowledge of future events."

[9] Hippolytus (*Dan. comm.* 2, 27, 4) says that this verse proves that God is immutable and unchangeable.

[10] *De Stoicorum repugnantiis* 38 (1051 E).

nonliving idols. This is the case in Romans and 1 Corinthians; it is also the case in 1 Thessalonians 1:9: Christians turn from idols to serve the "living and real God." In Galatians 4:8–10 the contrast is between the Creator and elemental spirits which he has created. Similarly in the apologetic Sibylline Oracles God is described as "immortal" as contrasted with idols (3, 276–78, 582, 600). This kind of contrast is also expressed at the end of 1 John (5:20–21): "We know that the Son of God has come and has given us understanding to know the true [God]; and we are in the true [God], in his Son Jesus Christ; he is the true God and eternal life. Children, keep yourselves from idols." A similar pattern is reflected in later Christian writers like Aristides, Theophilus, and Clement of Alexandria, who employ philosophical definitions against anthropomorphic idolatry.

These early Christian writers, then, while in every instance maintaining the primacy of faith in response to the self-revelation of God, do not hesitate to make use of the points of contact between God's revelation and the modes of expression prevalent in Hellenistic Judaism and in Graeco-Roman philosophy generally. This is especially the case in the Pauline epistles, even though the ultimate meaning of Paul's words, as at the beginning of Romans, is rather different from what a philosopher would have expected.[11] Men have knowledge of God, he says, only because God has revealed it to them (Rom. 1:19).

In the Pauline passages already cited, little is said

[11] See G. Bornkamm, *Das Ende des Gesetzes* (Munich, 1952), 9–33.

about the revelation of the Father through the Son, although it is probably implied in 1 Corinthians 8:6 ("through whom are all things"). To say that Christ is the agent or instrument of God in creation and in redemption is to say that he is the revelation of God as well (Col. 1:15–20), and this point, it would appear, is made when Paul uses language referring to the "image" of God. If Christ is "the image of the invisible God" (Col. 1:15), he is obviously the one through whom and in whom the Father is known.

The revelation of the Father to and through the Son is clearly set forth in a passage common to Matthew (11:25–27) and Luke (10:21–22). "No one knows the Father [or, who the Father is] but the Son," and the Son reveals the Father to others. The same point is more fully developed in the Gospel of John. No one has ever seen God; only the *Monogenes*, in the Father's bosom, has interpreted him (1:18; cf. 5:37). The only vision of God is the vision seen by Jesus, the one who is "from God" (6:46)—although the man who sees Jesus sees the Father (12:45; 14:9) because Jesus and the Father are one (10:30; cf. 10:38; 17:11). No one comes to the Father but through Jesus (14:6). John says nothing about knowledge of God in relation to the cosmos. Although the Word illuminates every man, when he came into the cosmos which was made through him the cosmos did not know him (1:9–10).

It may appear that there is a divergence between the affirmation, or some of the affirmations, of Paul and those of Jesus in the gospels. Ultimately, however, all the New Testament writers agree that God is known through his self-revelation, and that this self-revelation is the revelation of Christ. To be sure, in Romans 1:19ff. Paul does not speak explicitly of this revelation, but he does refer to the glory of the imperishable God —and with this passage we may compare 2 Corinthians 4:6: "God, who commanded the light to shine out of darkness, has shone in our hearts to give the knowledge of the glory of God in the face of Jesus Christ." Creation, redemption, and the revelation of the knowledge of God are thus combined in Paul's thought. In Romans 1:19ff. he does not explicitly refer to Christ because such a reference would not be germane to his argument.

We conclude that for the theologians of the earliest church all cosmological statements are ultimately Christological; the knowledge of God that man can infer from the cosmos by itself is inadequate and, apart from God's self-revelation in Christ, bound to lead to idolatry.

To put the point a little differently, there is no real knowledge of God apart from revelation; there is no knowledge of God apart from grace; there is no knowledge of God apart from faith. "In the wisdom of God, the world did not know God by wisdom" (1 Cor. 1:21).

At the same time, since Christian faith is not totally alien from rational constructions, the New Testament writers make use of terms which they share with some of their contemporaries. For them as for others, God is invisible, powerful, eternal, and imperishable. The popular philosophical terminology of causation can be employed in regard to him. It is fairly evident that all this language is secondary to, and derivative from, the primary affirmations of faith. But the fact that it could be employed at all left room for the development of various kinds of philosophical theologies.

THE EARLY SECOND CENTURY

When we come to the Christians who wrote in the period immediately after the apostolic age, we find reflections of philosophical theology not only in such a Hellenistic-Jewish-Christian author as Clement of Rome (end of the first century), who describes the harmonious operation of God's world in language based on Stoic models, but also in a letter written by Ignatius, bishop of Antioch early in the second century. For our purposes what Ignatius says is highly important, because behind it we can trace something of a tradition of philosophical thought. In his letter to Polycarp (3, 2) Ignatius speaks of Jesus Christ as "the eternal; the invisible, visible for us; the intangible; the impassible, passible for us; the one who endured for us in every way."[12] It is obvious that Ignatius' paradoxes come from a combination of language about God with language about Christ's passion. According to the New Testament and the philosophers, God is the one who is eternal, invisible, intangible, and impassible. According to the apostolic tradition Jesus was in time, visible, tangible, passible. Ignatius juxtaposes the terms and thus sets forth the paradoxical mystery of the incarnation.

---

[12] In his letter to the Smyrnaeans (3, 2), Ignatius states that Christ was tangible. Ignatius' word *apathēs*, "incapable of suffering" or "incapable of emotion," is very common in second-century philosophy and theology. See Appendix II.

But we can go behind what he says. He is opposing Christian Docetists, who held that, as God, the Christ could only have "seemed to suffer." They must be responsible for maintaining that Christ was eternal, invisible, intangible, and impassible. And behind their doctrine, in turn, there must lie the Christian theological doctrine of God. Therefore we must infer that in the church before Ignatius' time such language (1) had been currently used in regard to God the Father and (2) had next been applied to Christ as God. Ignatius reflects or creates the third stage of doctrinal development when he uses this language both of God the Father and of Christ but is also concerned to maintain the reality of the incarnation—which the Docetists had had to give up.

It is in the apocryphal *Preaching of Peter*[13] that we first encounter a specifically philosophical discussion of the one God. There we read that "there is one God, who made the beginning of all things and has control over their end." God is described as

> the invisible, who sees all things,
> uncontained, who contains all things,
> without needs, of whom all are in need and
>   because of whom they exist;
> incomprehensible, eternal, imperishable;
> unmade, who made all by the word of his power.

The negative adjectives reflect the popular philosophical theology found in contemporary writings both pagan and Jewish. "Invisible," "eternal," and "imperishable" are words used of God by Paul. In addition, the language of the *Preaching of Peter* is related not only to

[13] As quoted by Clement of Alexandria, *Str.* 6, 39, 2–3.

what God is not but to what he does: he sees all, contains all, and made all; all need him and owe their existence to him. I suggest that the negative adjectives provide a semi-philosophical framework for the positive doctrines, which are based on biblical and ecclesiastical tradition.

W. C. van Unnik has compared the theology of the *Preaching* and of Aristides with the theology expressed in such Gnostic documents as the *Apocryphon of John* and the *Sophia of Jesus Christ*. He argues that when the Gnostic authors claim that their theology is derived from revelation they have taken them from earlier Christian schools in which they were regarded as "expressions of a higher form of Christianity" (we have seen some evidence for this in Ignatius). He therefore suggests that both the *Preaching* and the Gnostic writings owe their theological formulations to Christian schools toward the beginning of the second century.[14]

I would express this a little differently, only because the statement by Ignatius places the "higher form" more toward the first century than the second. But I entirely agree with van Unnik that the decisive difference between Christian and Gnostic teaching lies not in the use or nonuse of various definitions but in the world views involved. For the Christian writers God is the transcendent Creator; for the Gnostics he is "the negation of this world and has practically nothing to do with it" (van Unnik).

In the *Apology* of Aristides we find the philosophical doctrines more fully developed. The author begins with two kinds of definitions, the first of which is both

[14] *Theologische Zeitschrift* 17 (1961), 166–74.

positive and Aristotelian: God is the unmoved Mover and Ruler of the universe, for "everything that moves is more powerful than what is moved, and that which rules is more powerful than what is ruled." This doctrine is an Aristotelian expression of the biblical doctrine of creation, and like the statements which follow really takes God's eternity and omnipotence for granted. Aristides also states that God is "by nature incomprehensible"; it might be better, and it would certainly be more consistent, to translate this phrase "incomprehensible as to his nature."

Actually Aristides knows a good deal. In the first place, God is eternal. He has no beginning (for what has a beginning has an end) and no end (for what has an end is destructible); he is therefore unbegotten, uncreated, immutable, and immortal. In the second place, he is perfect. He has no defects and no needs; he is not contained by anything but contains all things; he is therefore immobile, since he could not move from one place to another, and because he contains all he is immeasurable. He is neither male nor female (if he were, he would be subject to passion); he has no emotions such as anger or wrath (for none can resist him) or error or forgetting (since, positively, he is Wisdom and wholly Mind.[15] "He does not need sacrifice or libation."[16] He has no opponent, since no one is stronger than he is. In the third place, he has no name, form, or parts.

Aristides begins his work with these statements because he is going to attack the gods of the pagans as no

[15] For this remote echo of Xenophanes see page 26 below.
[16] Apparently a quotation from the Sibylline Oracles (8, 390).

gods at all. Presumably he is following a pattern provided in earlier apologetic, either Jewish or Christian, since he is hardly a philosophical thinker. He attacks the gods of others as subject to suffering and death but simply states that the Lord Jesus Christ is "the Son of God Most High, who came down from heaven and assumed flesh of the Virgin" (15, 1). He does not see any of the difficulties which Ignatius had already faced. For this reason his work may be even more valuable. It is hardly an original creation but probably reflects teaching current in the church in his day.

Indeed, with his statements we may well compare the first Mandate of the *Shepherd* of Hermas. There we find the injunction to "believe that God is one, who created, completed, and made everything out of the nonexistent for existence, and contains everything, being alone uncontained." Here again the unusual semi-philosophical language suggests that this mandate is not Hermas' own but reflects common Jewish-Christian teaching prevalent in the early second-century church.

From the middle of the second century we possess a fascinating, if somewhat stylized, account of a pagan's search for God in the philosophical schools. This is the story provided by the Graeco-Samaritan Justin, and told by him to the Hellenistic Jewish teacher Trypho (*Dial.* 2ff.). At the beginning, says Justin, when he wanted to be a disciple of some one of the philosophers, he first turned to a Stoic teacher and spent considerable time with him. From the Stoic he learned nothing about God. His teacher did not possess such knowledge and, as teachers sometimes do, claimed that it was unnecessary. We may add that the teacher was evidently not an up-to-date Stoic like Epictetus, for whom the question of God was deeply significant; instead, he was evidently an old-fashioned, orthodox Stoic, transmitting the traditional view according to which theology was a subdivision of physics. After Justin left the Stoic he turned to a Peripatetic, but from him he learned nothing at all. A third try brought Justin to a Pythagorean who, he says, was convinced of his own wisdom. Insisting on the prerequisites for his course, which Justin did not have, the teacher sent Justin away.

Justin's dealings with three philosophers had disappointed him profoundly, and it was not for some time that he approached another. Like any other literate person in the second century, he had heard of the fame of the Platonists, and when a new teacher came to Samaria he decided to try once more. With him, he says, "I advanced and greatly improved day by day. The knowledge of incorporeal objects came over me, and the contemplation of the ideas gave wings to my mind; I thought that in a short time I had become wise, and I stupidly hoped that I would have the vision of God—for this is the goal of the philosophy of Plato." In the religious-minded Platonism of the second century he had finally found a spiritual home—or so he thought.

One day, however, he was taking a walk and silently meditating when an old man came along and engaged him in conversation concerning his favorite themes. Very soon Justin found himself in a discussion of the knowledge of God. When the old man asked him for a definition of God, Justin set forth the usual school statement: "That which is uniformly and consistently always the same and provides the cause of existence for

all other beings." The old man agreed. As it turns out
later, he is a Christian, and the ground of his agreement
therefore lies in the common Christian philosophical
theology of the time. But the Christian is not concerned
so much with this acceptable definition as with the
question as to how God is known. God, he says, is not
really known by the philosophers because he is not
perceptible to the senses. As a Platonist of sorts, Justin
claims that "the divine is not visible to the eyes but is
comprehensible only to the mind, as Plato said."[17]

"So there is a special power in our mind? . . . Or
will the mind of man ever see God unless it is adorned
with Holy Spirit?"

"Plato says that there is an eye of the mind. If it is
pure, by it we are able to see that which is, the cause of
all things, which has no color or form or size or any
quality the eye sees. Being itself, above all essence
(*ousia*),[18] inexpressible and inexplicable, alone beautiful
and good, suddenly appears to souls of a good nature
because of their kinship and desire for vision."

Justin's statement leads the old man to question the
whole basis of the Platonic doctrine of the vision of
God. "What kinship do we have with God? Is the soul
divine and immortal and a part of that 'royal Mind?'[19]
When it sees God, is the result that with our mind we
contain the divine and from it become blessed?" Justin
affirms that this is so, and then the old man proceeds to
use the Peripatetic arguments—which, as we have seen,
Justin had never encountered—against the innate im-

[17] *Phaedo* 65e–66a; cf. Maximus of Tyre, *Diss.* 17, 9 (cited by
Otto *ad loc.*).   [18] *Rep.* vii. 509b.   [19] *Philebus* 30d.

mortality of the soul and the Platonic doctrines of reminiscence and transmigration.[20] At the end of the discussion Justin's Platonism was shattered and he gladly turned to study of the Old Testament revelation, through which he came to Christianity.

This sketch of Justin's conversion shows us how important, at least for some Christians, the role of philosophy was in the second century. It did not lead directly to Christian faith, which was the consequence of revelation alone. It did, however, stimulate men's minds and (as employed by the old man) lead to recognition of its own problems, to which revelation could be regarded as giving an answer. In addition, as we saw at the beginning of the recorded conversation, theological philosophy and philosophical theology shared a common understanding of two cardinal attributes of God. First, he is immutable, hence uncreated and eternal and imperishable. Second, he is the ultimate cause of all things or, one might say, the ground of being. It is to be noted that as the conversation proceeded the old Christian criticized the mode of Justin's religious knowledge but not the content of what he knew. He had no complaint to make when Justin said that God is Being itself, above all essence, inexpressible, inexplicable. This philosophical doctrine was also the common Christian theological doctrine.

As a Christian teacher, Justin defines God just as he defined him when he was a Platonist: God is eternally immutable and the source of all existence (*Dial.* 3, 5;

[20] Cf. my article, "Aristotle and the Conversion of Justin," *Journal of Theological Studies* 7 (1956), 246–48.

Apol. 1, 13, 4). He has no name, for a name is applied by someone "elder" than the one named; his appelations are derived from his relations with man and the cosmos (*Apol.* 2, 6, 1). Justin absolutely rejects a literal interpretation of biblical metaphors: God does not have hands, feet, fingers, or soul, for he is not composite (*Dial.* 114, 3); he is not moved nor does he walk, sleep, or wake. Though he can be said to be "in the heavens" or "above heaven" or "above the universe," he is not really located in space at all (*Dial.* 127, 3).[21] Similarly Justin's sometime disciple Tatian insists upon the strictest transcendentalist monotheism; his ideas are closely parallel to those of Middle Platonists and in explicit opposition to those of the Stoics.[22] The same view is expressed by Theophilus of Antioch. The form of God is "ineffable and inexpressible" and his so-called "names" refer to his powers (*Ad Autol.* 1, 3); he is actually without beginning because he does not come into existence and he is immutable because immortal (1, 4). Furthermore, there is no difference between the theology of the apologists and that of contemporary Gnostics such as the Valentinians; in the "Great Notice" of Ptolemaeus we find the adjectives "uncontainable," "invisible," "eternal," "ungenerated," and so on.[23] Hippolytus claimed that aspects of the Valentinian doctrine of God were Pythagorean (*Ref.* 6, 29, 2); he might have added that they were shared with Platonic philosophers and Christian apologists as well.

[21] "In," *Dial.* 127, 5; 129, 1; "above heaven," 56, 1; 60, 2; "above the universe," 60, 5. See E. R. Goodenough, *The Theology of Justin Martyr* (Jena, 1923), 122–38, especially 126.
[22] M. Elze, *Tatian und seine Theologie* (Göttingen, 1960), 63–69.
[23] Irenaeus, *Adv. haer.* 1, 1, 1ff.

Before we go on to say more about Christian theology, we should briefly consider the nature of the philosophical doctrine of God in the second century. Among the most important witnesses to it is Albinus, a Middle Platonist who wrote his *Introduction* toward the middle of the century. He states that the "first God" is "eternal, ineffable, perfect in himself (i.e., without needs), ever-perfect (i.e., forever perfect), complete (i.e., completely perfect): deity, being, truth, symmetry, the good." Albinus insists that he is not really defining this transcendent being, but he goes on to state that "he is ineffable because comprehensible by the mind alone, as it is said, since he has no genus or form or differentia, nor has anything taken place to him, either evil or good."[24] The human mind can reach him only in three ways: by abstraction or negation, by analogy, or by gradual ascension.[25] It is evident that Albinus is using school definitions, for we find very similar ideas in the treatise *De Platone* by Apuleius. God is incorporeal, alone immeasurable, the founder and constructor of all things, blessed and beatific, supremely good, in need of nothing but himself holding all together; celestial, ineffable, unnameable, invisible, undominated.[26] Similar points are made by the anti-Christian writer Celsus. God has no form like anything else; he does not participate in shape or color or movement, or even in being; all things are derived from him, while he

---

[24] Albinus, *Didasc.* 10 (pp. 164–65 Hermann).

[25] R. E. Witt, *Albinus and the History of Middle Platonism* (Cambridge, 1937), 132; cf. A.-J. Festugière, *La révélation d'Hermès Trismégiste*, IV (Paris, 1954), 92–102.

[26] *De Platone* 1, 5 (p. 86 Thomas [cf. Witt, *op. cit.*, 99]).

is derived from nothing.[27] Celsus goes beyond Albinus, however, by insisting that God is not attainable by reason. He agrees with Apuleius that God cannot be given a name.[28]

All these writers are Platonists, but it is evident that in essentials their teaching was accepted by the general run of Stoics. Diogenes Laertius, summarizing Stoic doctrine, states that God is an immortal rational living being, perfect or intelligent in blessedness, not receptive of any evil, taking providential care of the cosmos and what is in the cosmos; he is not in any respect anthropomorphic. He is the Demiurge of all things and, so to speak, the Father of all, in general and in particular permeating all things. He is given many appellations in relation to his powers."[29] This description sounds quite Platonic, but there is one significant difference. The pronoun we have translated as masculine must really be translated as neuter, for to the Stoics God was definitely not to be called "he" but "it." Their God was not so much ineffable as impersonal, and Christians could hardly make much use of such a theology. We refer to it only to show how many points of contact there were among the various schools.[30]

Indeed, just as Philo had traced back his own philosophy to Moses, so in the second century another Philo, this one of Byblos, ascribed contemporary theology to

[27] Origen, *Contra Celsum* 6, 63–64.
[28] *Ibid.*, 6, 65; compare Clement as discussed below.
[29] Diogenes Laertius 7, 147 (H. von Arnim, *Stoicorum veterum fragmenta* [Leipzig, 1905–24], II, 1021).
[30] We shall discuss the theology of Numenius of Apamea in the third essay.

Zoroaster. Relying on a document called the *Sacred Assembly*, he stated that according to Zoroaster God is "the first, imperishable, eternal, uncreated, without parts, most unlike anything else, supporter of all good, in need of no gifts, best of all goods, wisest of all the wise; he is the Father of lawfulness and justice, taught by himself, natural and perfect, the sole discoverer of what is sacred and natural."[31] These examples indicate the universality of a general philosophical theology.[32]

When we turn back to Christian writers of the later second century, we find philosophy constantly being pressed into the service of Christian theology. Athenagoras, for example, insists that God is ungenerated, invisible, impassible, incomprehensible, and immeasurable. He is known, as Albinus had said, only by mind and reason. But by "mind and reason" Athenagoras means not simply the mind and reason of man, but the Mind and Reason of God, which he identifies with the Son of God. Christian teaching about God is in harmony with what the philosophers, or some of them, taught, but it transcends their teaching. As he says, one cannot say anything positive about the Father except on the basis of the revelation given through the prophets, who were moved by the divine Spirit (*Leg.* 9, 1). Christian doctrine is ultimately not of human origin but oracular, derived from God (11, 1). It must be ad-

---

[31] Eusebius, *Praeparatio Evangelica* 1, 10, 52; cf. J. Bidez and F. Cumont, *Les mages hellénisés* (Paris, 1938), II, 157.

[32] Hippolytus (*Ref.* 4, 43, 4) ascribes a similar—actually Neopythagorean—doctrine to the Egyptians. On the general idea of "ancient oriental wisdom" see my *The Letter and the Spirit* (London, 1957), 1–30.

mitted, however, that in spite of these assertions he does make use of philosophical models when he tries to prove the unity of God.[33]

Similarly Irenaeus, who insists on theological grounds that God is uncontainable, incomprehensible, and invisible—and known only through his Son—makes use of the doctrine of Xenophanes that God is entirely seeing, entirely knowing, entirely hearing; and like the Platonists he insists that God is the source of all good things. In his view, "religious and devout men" of every nation could speak of God in this way, while the same view of God is contained in the scriptures.[34] This is to say that God's revelation is not completely confined to scripture or tradition. Irenaeus understands his Bible in the light of philosophical theology and, in part, vice versa.

A more fully philosophical theology is set forth by Clement of Alexandria, partly because he makes so much use of Philo. Clement insisted upon the monadic unity of God and described him as ineffable and invisible. In a key passage (*Str.* 2, 81, 4–6) he went beyond Philo to show how impossible it is to make positive statements about God. Since God is the cause prior to the origination and existence of all other beings, it must be held that he cannot be assigned genus, differentia, species, individuation, number, accident, or substance. He has no parts because the one is indivisible; he is therefore infinite, shapeless, and unnameable. E. F. Osborn has related this statement to the *Parmenides* of

[33] On this proof see Appendix I.
[34] See R. M. Grant in *Wolfson Jubilee Volumes* (Jerusalem, 1965), 376–79.

Plato,[35] but it is unlikely that Clement was acquainted with this dialogue. His writings seem to contain only one possible allusion to it, and there Clement is expressing a doctrine not Platonic but Middle Platonist.[36] The categories Clement is using are Aristotelian as mediated by some Middle Platonist teacher such as Albinus. Indeed, Albinus provides a statement very close to that of Clement. The first God is "ineffable and conceivable only by the mind, since there is no genus or species or differentia or accident"; he cannot be described as evil or good or active or inactive.[37]

Like Albinus, Clement draws negative conclusions from his negative principles. God has no "shape, motion, immobility, throne, place, right or left side" (*Str.* 5, 71, 4); indeed, he cannot properly be called "one or the good or the one itself or Father or God or Demiurge or Lord" (5, 82, 1). God is really "unknown," as Paul said in Acts 17:23. He can be known not by the work of human reason but only by divine grace (5, 82, 4) in the revelation of the Son (4, 156, 1). Thus Clement goes beyond Middle Platonism and reflects the standpoint less of the New Testament than of Philo of Alexandria, who had written that God can be comprehended only by himself (*Praem.* 40).

There is a surprising parallel between what Clement says of the hidden nature of God and what the earlier Alexandrian Gnostic Basilides taught about the same

[35] *The Philosophy of Clement of Alexandria* (Cambridge, 1957), 29 (he does not suggest that Clement had actually read the *Parmenides*).

[36] "The idea is a thought of God" (*Str.* 5, 16, 3; cf. *Parmenides* 132b). On the theory cf. Witt, *op. cit.*, 70–75.

[37] *Eisag.* 10 (p. 165, 4–10 Hermann).

subject. According to Basilides too, God cannot be described in terms of genus, species, and substance.[38] But Basilides boldly proceeded to claim that one should therefore speak of God as nonexistent. In his view, "the non-existent God made the non-existent cosmos out of the non-existent." The difference between Basilides and Clement, however, is more crucial than the similarity. Basilides is a Gnostic. This is to say that God can be *known* through the Gnostic theology. He is actually equivalent to the negations of the *via negativa·* For Clement, on the other hand, God transcends these limiting statements as grace transcends reason or nature. The Gnostic Basilides knows. Clement, though he values knowledge highly, believes—in God.

PHILOSOPHICAL THEOLOGY AND ITS LIMITS

The greatest of the Alexandrian theologians was not Clement, however, but Origen, and when we consider the development of early Christian theology we have to take Origen's own development into account. In a relatively early though exceedingly influential treatise *On First Principles* Origen followed the path cut out by the apologists and Clement, going so far as to define God as "a unified intellectual being (*natura*), permitting of absolutely no addition in himself, so that it may not be believed that he has either anything greater or anything lesser in himself, but that he is in every way a monad and, so to speak, a henad."[39] On this basis it was

[38] Hippolytus, *Ref.* 7, 15.
[39] *De princ.* 1, 1, 6 (p. 21 Koetschau).

inevitable that he should say that God is completely impassible; he lacks all emotions.[40] In another relatively early work, the *Commentary on John*, Origen not only insisted upon divine impassibility, on the ground of divine immutability,[41] but also drew ethical consequences from this doctrine. Sexual enthusiasm within marriage can be accepted only by those who have "thrown away the words of God about impassibility."[42]

In a homily on Numbers (*Num. hom.* 16, 3 [p. 139 Baehrens]) Origen reiterated his stand, interpreting Numbers 23:19 in the Greek version—"God is not like a man"—to mean that God is impassible.[43] By the time he had delivered further sermons on Numbers, however, the ice began to break up, though rather slowly. God rejoices over the salvation of men and grieves over them as well, though "all the passages in which God is said to grieve or rejoice or hate or be glad must be understood as spoken by the scripture allegorically (*tropicē*) and in human fashion. For the divine nature is far removed from every feeling of emotion and alteration; it always remains motionless and unperturbed, on the summit of blessedness."[44] Origen has already said that God rejoices and grieves, but he cannot relate this

[40] *Ibid.*, 2, 4, 4 (p. 131).   [41] Fragment 51 (p. 526 Preuschen).
[42] *Ioh. comm.* 20, 36 (p. 376).
[43] Here he follows the tradition of Philo: *Somn.* 1, 237; *Immut.* 54; *Quaest. in Gen.* 2, 54 (cf. H. A. Wolfson, *Philo* [Cambridge, Mass., 1947], II, 97). It should be noted, however, that though Philo says that God is described as rejoicing or being angry so that readers of the Bible can be educated away from literalism (*Somn.* 2, 176–79; see note 47 below), he also says that a reference to God's mercy in Genesis 33:11 is "both dogmatic and instructive" (*Sacr.* 42) and explicitly states that God shows mercy (*Mos.* 1, 198). For other references cf. Wolfson, *Philo*, II 258 and 412.
[44] *Num. hom.* 23, 2 (pp. 211–14 Baehrens).

idea to his philosophical-theological framework. He must therefore hold that language about rejoicing and believing has been used in scripture for the instruction of simpler believers.

In a very late homily on Ezekiel, Origen finally changed his mind. He was already willing to write in regard to the Son that "the impassible one suffered by being compassionate."[45] Now on Ezekiel he stated that only a hard-hearted man is unmoved when he is asked to take pity on someone; the Saviour, however, was actually moved by men's petitions. Indeed, the whole story of the incarnation is a proof of this. First the Saviour was moved by compassion; then he descended and appeared among men. He experienced the passion or emotion of love.

Moreover, does not the Father and God of the universe somehow experience emotion, since he is long-suffering and of great mercy? Or do you not know that when he distributes human gifts he experiences human emotion? For "the Lord your God endured your ways, as when a man endures his son" [Deut. 1:31]. Therefore God endures our ways, just as the Son of God bears our emotions. The Father himself is not impassible. If he is asked, he takes pity and experiences grief, he suffers something of love and he comes to be in a situation in which, because of the greatness of his nature, he cannot be and for our sake he experiences human emotion (*humanas sustinet passiones*).[46]

This is a very remarkable passage not only in relation to Origen's earlier statements but also in relation to the whole Alexandrian theological tradition. Philo had quoted a rather similar passage from Deuteronomy

---

[45] *Matt. comm.* 10, 23 (p. 33, 3 Klostermann).
[46] *Ezech. hom.* 6, 6 (pp. 384–85 Baehrens).

(8:5) but had carefully chosen one in which the word "instruct" occurred, so that he could explain anthropomorphism as educational.[47] Origen uses a different passage and combines it with echoes of Exodus 34:6: "the Lord God is merciful and takes pity, long-suffering and of great mercy and true." Pohlenz claimed that Origen was speaking merely pedagogically and that this passage does not reflect his real view.[48] It would appear, on the contrary, that something of great theological significance has happened here.

Conceivably Origen has been influenced by the language of Ignatius, who frequently spoke of the suffering of Christ, his God, and even of the passion of God; for in several of the late homilies Origen alludes to Ignatian phrases. Clearly an early Christian could speak of God's suffering when he referred to the suffering of the Son. Ignatius was followed by Tatian, who called Christ "the God who suffered,"[49] and Clement spoke of Christ not only as "the God who suffered" but also as "the God who washed men's feet."[50] These authors, however, were speaking of the paradoxical mystery of the Incarnation, not of the nature of God as God. What Origen has finally done is to give more weight to the revelation of God in Christ than to the negative conceptions provided by philosophical theology. We do not know how he would have related the two frames of reference

[47] *Immut.* 54; *Somn.* 1, 237; *Quaest. in Gen.* 2, 54 (cf. Wolfson, *Philo*, II, 129—but the reference is to Deut. 8:5, not 1:31). Clement also quotes the verse among others on *paideia* (*Str.* 1, 172, 2).

[48] *Vom Zorne Gottes* (Göttingen, 1909), 36.

[49] *Orat.* 13 (p. 15, 5 Schwartz).

[50] *Protr.* 106, 4; *Paed.* 2, 38, 1. On the other hand, impassibility is emphasized in the *Stromata*, written for the more mature Gnostic Christian.

had he continued to develop his theology. All we can say is that an authentically Christian insight has appeared and that it was bound to have drastic consequences.

In the thought of the earlier writers we have discussed, and in Origen's thought as well, there is a healthy recognition of the limits of philosophical theology and a firm insistence upon the absolute transcendence of God. What is often lacking (though not, for example, in Irenaeus) is an equally clear affirmation of faith in the revelation of God through Christ. If God was known through his self-revelation in his Son, surely our knowledge of him does not consist solely of the *via negativa*. It must involve some recognition of God's love for mankind. There must be what Charles Hartshorne has called "dipolar theism." As H. D. McDonald says, "While we are quite prepared to affirm belief in God as being without 'body and parts,' we hesitate when we come to add 'and passions.' "[51] It may be possible to relate this hesitation to the *via negativa* itself. By means of the negative attributes, it may be claimed, ancient theologians were trying to claim that God was in no way inferior to man, and they regarded "passions" as somehow subhuman. With a more adequate understanding of human psychology we do not share their view of the emotions, and therefore we do not need to agree with them that God is absolutely impassible.[52]

Perhaps a little more should be said about early

[51] *Harvard Theological Review* 58 (1965), 415–16.

[52] See Appendix II for a more complete discussion. It should be said that Clement could indicate that out of love for man God did condescend to the passions when the Word of God became man (*Paed.* 1, 74, 4).

Christian theology in general. There are many difficulties in it, and little emphasis has been laid on them here. One of the most troublesome may lie in the rather philosophical notion of God as the primal cause. We are not accustomed to assign only one cause to the events we know, and the ancient classifications of causes are no longer viable. For this reason, among others, we should not claim that the specific doctrines of ancient theologians are permanently valid. All we should claim is that the approach which the early fathers used is still significant. They began from Christian faith but did not hesitate to use the philosophical language, and some of the philosophical structures, of their day. Indeed, in their eclectic thought we encounter not only the Platonic views which we have emphasized but also ideas taken from Scepticism, Stoicism, and Aristotelianism. The only philosophy of their day which they were unwilling to use was Epicureanism, and their antagonism toward it was due partly to the fact that it was crudely materialistic and partly to the bad reputation which Epicureans had among other philosophers. Christians actually joined Epicureans in their attack on pagan polytheism and superstition.

It sometimes comes as something of a shock when we recognize that Christians were not at all averse to using arguments derived from the Sceptics. We might have expected that they would do so when they confronted the myths about the gods or the widespread belief in astrology and cosmic fatalism. But the influence of Scepticism goes deeper. Some Sceptics argued that since absolute knowledge, especially of the future, is impossible, and since men must act, they must act on the basis of probabilities. The judgment of what is probable they called *pistis*. For Christians, *pistis* meant primarily what we call "faith," both belief and trust in God and, as well, obedience to his will. There was a point of contact, and quite a few theologians of the early church proceeded to interpret Christian faith in Sceptical terms. *Pistis*, says one of them, takes the lead in all human actions. When you plant seeds you "entrust" them to the ground; when you sail in a boat you have "faith" in the boat and the pilot; when you get married and bring up children you are living with faith, confidence, or hope that things will turn out well.[53]

In relation to the doctrine of God, then, what the early Christian theologians show us is that by continuing along some of the lines marked out in the New Testament and by making more explicit use of philosophical ideas they tried to work out some of the implications of the basic self-revelation of God—in terms adequate for their own times. They began with faith (which they interpreted philosophically too[54]) and used philosophy as a language of interpretation. Because they continued to recognize that God could not be contained in the philosophical terminology, they remained open to fresh insights and new ways of explanation. Origen's ideas provide a conspicuous example of

[53] Theophilus, *Ad Autol.* 1, 8; cf. Clitomachus in Cicero, *Lucull.* 99 and 109; Sextus Empiricus, *Pyrrh. hypot.* 2, 244. Other Christian parallels: *Sexti Sententiae* 166 (p. 32 Chadwick); Origen, *Contra Celsum* 1, 10–11; Eusebius, *P.E.* 1, 5, 5–6.

[54] On various other views of faith cf. H. A. Wolfson, *The Philosophy of the Church Fathers*, I (Cambridge, Mass., 1956), 102–40.

this openness. Such an approach, I believe, provides something of a model even today.

It is more than an approach, however, in at least one regard. When we recall the way in which Origen's mind was moved as he meditated on the revelation of God's love, we must ask with Bishop Nygren if Ignatius did not firmly appropriate certain basic Christian insights about God as love, even though these insights were later distorted.[55] Ignatius wrote that "the beginning is faith, but the end is love" (*Eph.* 14, 1) and also that "the whole is faith and love" (*Smyrn.* 6, 2). The point is made even more simply in 1 John 4:8: "He who does not love has not known God, for God is love."

On this crucial doctrine some of the Christian Gnostics were in agreement with their more orthodox contemporaries. According to the Valentinians described by Hippolytus, "the Father was alone ungenerated, without place or time, without counsellor or any other being that can be thought of in any way. He was isolated and at rest, himself alone in himself. But since he was productive, it seemed good to him to generate and bring forth what he had in himself that was most beautiful and most perfect; for he was not devoted to isolation. For he was wholly love, and love is not love unless there is something loved."[56] Here is a radical

---

[55] A. Nygren, *Agape and Eros* (rev. trans.; London, 1953), 261; cf. J. Colson, "Agapé chez Saint-Ignace d'Antioche," *Texte und Untersuchungen* 78 (Berlin, 1961), 341–53. For a different but analogous appreciation of Ignatius cf. R. Bultmann, "Ignatius und Paulus," in *Studia Paulina J. de Zwaan* (Haarlem, 1953), 37–51.

[56] Hippolytus, *Ref.* 6, 29, 5–6. The passage is less Christian than it sounds, for it is based, as Hippolytus points out, on a form of

monotheism in which some questions are begged (how was the Father love, then, unless the Son was eternally generated or the world was eternal?) and the emanation of the aeons is immediately described as what the Father produced. Yet the impulse which led the Valentinians to make this statement is surely Christian in origin and, in part, in expression. Gnostics and Christians at their best agreed that God must ultimately be described in terms not only of power and judgment but of love, a love made known and expressed through grace.

---

number symbolism according to which the number "one" is "productive" of other numbers; for generative productivity see also A. D. Nock and A.-J. Festugière, *Corpus Hermeticum*, IV (Paris, 1954), 132: a Hermetic fragment according to which the Logos is the productive agent. On the other hand, the mention of the Father as "love" is probably based on something like the tradition reflected in 1 John 4:8 and 16.

THE SON OF GOD

WE ARE so accustomed to the traditional language of the Christian Church that we think it is perfectly natural to find Jesus called "Son of God" and "Son of Man" in the early Christian books, and to have these titles explained as referring to his divine nature (Son of God) and his human nature (Son of Man). These titles are not as simple as they look. In the Jewish literature of the first century, the title "Son of God" is actually used of human beings. A fragment from the Dead Sea Scrolls speaks of the Messiah, a man chosen by God, as "Son of God"; and in the apocalyptic book of Enoch there is a supernatural, heavenly figure who is called "Son of Man."

This example should warn us against thinking that we can have some kind of "instant understanding" of what the titles assigned to Jesus by the early church really meant. They are more strange and complicated than we assume they are.

But before we can say anything about the titles, we should consider what it is that we know about Jesus. By "know" I do not refer to religious intuitions of what he has meant to Christians or what he can mean to us. This kind of meaning is supremely important to his followers. But since not all men follow him, and since Christians claim that his life was a human life, of the kind we know from biographies and autobiographies, we should begin with the kind of picture which is based on generally accepted information. To be sure, this is not the kind of picture we find in the gospels. The gospels were written by believers for believers; they are written from the standpoint of faith in Jesus. But in the early church there were different modes of faith, reflected in the gospels; there were different levels of understanding of the meaning of Jesus. Moreover, the early Christians were aware that to some extent the traditions about the ministry of Jesus, in Galilee and Jerusalem, were different from their own teaching about his meaning as the risen Lord. They were honest enough to retain many of the old traditions, and for this reason it is possible for us to recover something of the history of his life. Striking examples of this honesty occur in the Gospel of Mark, where we often read that the disciples did not understand what he said to them. One can argue that Mark believes he knows more than the disciples did; but even if this is so, the fact that he preserves a record of their ignorance shows that he is aware of a difference between the earlier viewpoint and the later one. In the Gospel of Luke we read that at one point "they believed that the kingdom of God would immediately appear" (Luke 19:11). Luke knows that it did not appear in this way, but he is willing to record the fact that they thought it would. All I am suggesting is that there are some historical facts or memories in the gospels and that it is therefore possible to go behind the evangelists toward Jesus himself.

What we know about Jesus is quite a bit. He proclaimed the coming of the reign of God and believed that it had at least been inaugurated in his own mission. He cast out demons and healed the sick as signs of the beginning of God's reign. He taught men, mostly in parables, about the need for taking a stand on his side and God's. Above all, they were to reciprocate God's love for them by loving others. He took a rather free attitude toward the religious law of his time and ate indiscriminately with tax collectors and sinners. He gathered a few disciples around him and went up to Jerusalem to proclaim the kingdom there. After breaking bread with his disciples at a last supper, he was seized by the authorities and soon crucified. His disciples knew that he was dead, but they also were convinced that God raised him from the dead and that his spirit was present among them. Empowered by this spirit, as they said, they continued to proclaim his significance, at first only to their fellow Jews, later to everyone who would listen.

There is one significant change in the proclamation. Whereas for Jesus himself its center lay in the reign of

God and concerned his own activity only secondarily, for his followers the center came to lie in Jesus, although they did not stop proclaiming the coming of the kingdom. Thus while Jesus laid emphasis primarily on the present and the future, his disciples gradually came to lay the emphasis first on past, present, and future, and then chiefly on past and present. The emphasis on God's future action diminished. Whereas the earliest Christians had expected the future to come to them, later Christians came to think of themselves as entering the future, individually, at death.

The changes we have been mentioning were accompanied by reinterpretations of the meaning of Jesus. As the one who proclaimed the coming of God's reign, his followers called him "Son of Man" or "Messiah" (the title "Messiah" in Hebrew or Aramaic becomes "Christos" or "Christ" in Greek).[1] In these titles em-

---

[1] The titles "Son of Man" and "Christ" conveyed little meaning to Christians in the Graeco-Roman world. (1) "Son of Man" is fairly common in the canonical gospels, but outside them in the New Testament it occurs only in Acts 7:56 ("like a son of man" in Revelation 1:13 and 14:14 is directly from Daniel 7:13). Ignatius (*Eph.* 20, 2) refers the phrase to the human nature of Jesus, who is "son of man and Son of God," and Barnabas 12, 10 says that he is "not son of man but Son of God." The term appealed to the Gnostic imagination, and an archetypal Son of Man is to be found among the Sethian-Ophites (Irenaeus, *Adv. haer.* 1, 30, 1 and 5 [pp. 227 and 232 Harvey]), the Naassenes (Hippolytus, *Ref.* 5, 6, 3; 5, 7, 33), the Valentinians (Irenaeus, *Adv. haer.* 1, 12, 4, pp. 113–14; 1, 15, 3, pp. 150–51; Hippolytus, *Ref.* 6, 51, 4; Origen, *Ioh. comm.* 13, 4 [p. 276 Preuschen]), and the followers of Monoimus (Hippolytus, *Ref.* 8, 12, 2ff.). It is absent from the writings of the Greek apologists and Clement of Alexandria, while Irenaeus (e.g., *Adv. haer.* 5, 21, 1, p. 381) and Origen (e.g., *De princ.* 2, 6, 3 [p. 143 Koetschau]) once more refer it to Jesus' human nature. (2) "Christ" is a proper name in the Pauline epistles, while in the gospels it is interpreted in relation to "Son of God" (e.g., Mark

phasis is laid on his present role and its culmination in a future reign. Next, it would appear, he was called "Lord" and "Son of God"; finally, as we shall see, the implications of these names were more fully worked out.

When we begin with Jesus and his mission and his disciples we are in a setting in which he is obviously completely human. From the beginning the church insisted upon his humanity, and the earlier gospels make this point absolutely clear. We might suppose that the stories of his miracles would detract from his humanity, but since similar stories were told of heroes and even of philosophers in the ancient world it is evident that though they point beyond humanity (toward God the creator and sustainer of men) they do so only *through* humanity. Sometimes the disciples of Jesus address him, indeed, as "rabbi." This term of address clearly shows that they regarded him as belonging to a well-defined category of teachers in the Jewish world.

He himself prayed to God and taught his disciples to pray. He was devoted to God, the heavenly Father of whom both he and his disciples were sons. At one point in the gospel story a man addressed him as "Good master," and he asked him, "Why do you call me good? No one is good but God alone." This is the way the saying reads in the Gospel of Mark; the evangelist Matthew shows us how early Christian reverence sometimes modified the sayings of Jesus, for in his gospel Jesus asks, "Why do you ask me about what is good?"

14:61; Matt. 16:16; John 20:31). For Irenaeus' use of both terms cf. A. Houssiau, *La christologie de saint Irénée* (Louvain, 1955), 27 and 37–38.

It is clear enough, however, that in the original saying God was differentiated from man, and Jesus identified himself as man.

We should not speak of Jesus as "merely man" or "just a man." To speak thus would be to neglect the uniqueness and the potentialities of human existence. According to the Old Testament, the Bible of Jesus and his disciples, God made man in his own image. Nothing in creation except the angels is as close to God as man is.[2] And it would appear that in Jesus' own teaching he referred to this Old Testament doctrine. His opponents were asking him about the payment of tribute to the Romans, and he asked them whose image and likeness was on a coin one of them had. Obviously it was the Roman emperor's. But then he went on to tell them, "Give what is Caesar's to Caesar and what is God's to God." If the sequence is logical, it implies that as the coin bearing Caesar's image belongs to him, so man, who bears God's image, belongs to God. What seems to differentiate Jesus from other men in the earlier Christian traditions is his wholehearted devotion to God. He could reiterate the Old Testament teaching about love toward God; more important, he could exemplify it. On the cross, it is said, he cried out in the words of Psalm 22:1, "My God, my God, why have you forsaken me?" It may be that the tradition has imaginatively ascribed these words to him, but anyone who invented such a scene would have had to possess a measure of creative boldness which goes well beyond what we know of Jesus' followers. If he uttered these words, as I believe he did, it is clear that he was expressing, and

[2] Cf. also Matt. 6:28; Luke 12:24.

presumably experiencing, a deep sense of alienation from God. Again his humanity is reflected. At the same time, he still addresses God as "*my* God." The humanity is filled with a faithful obedience which, in the Christian view, is unique.

This is to say that the starting point for the Christian theological views of Jesus lies within the ministry of the man Jesus of Nazareth, and in the responses of his earliest disciples to him. Christology is not simply an importation from outside; it is rooted not only in faith but also in history, or rather in an inseparable combination of the two. Perhaps it would be better, however, to say that this was one of the starting points. The other was surely the disciples' conviction that this Jesus who had been crucified had now been raised from the dead and was exalted at God's right hand. Few Christian convictions have caused as much difficulty as this one has. Among the Christians at Corinth, as early as the year 55, we find those who doubt the possibility of resurrection. According to the Gospel of Matthew, critics were arguing that the disciples of Jesus had stolen his body from its tomb. Later writers and modern ones as well have found the Christian stories of the resurrection incredible, and the Christian defensive arguments have never been especially convincing. I should certainly hesitate to use the claim of Tertullian that it is certain because it is impossible. To me it seems that the basic apostolic conviction was that Jesus was somehow alive among them and that, if this was so, God had indeed acted and had raised him and exalted him. The various stories of appearances, on this view, represent attempts by Christians to define the indefinable, to express the ineffable. They are the products of a conviction and are wrongly used to produce, or reproduce, the conviction. That to which they point is the exaltation of Jesus, and I believe that we can see this exaltation clearly expressed in two texts of the New Testament.

The first occurs in a sermon ascribed to the apostle Peter. "Let all the house of Israel know assuredly that God has made him both Lord and Messiah, this Jesus whom you crucified" (Acts 2:36). Here it is plain that "Jesus of Nazareth"—as Peter has earlier called him (Acts 2:22)—has become both Lord and Messiah in consequence of God's act after the crucifixion. The second text occurs at the beginning of Paul's letter to the Romans, where he is setting forth the common early Christian faith in writing to a church whose members he does not know personally. He describes "the gospel of God" as "the gospel concerning his Son, who has descended from David according to the flesh and designated Son of God in power according to the Spirit of holiness by his resurrection from the dead, Jesus Christ our Lord" (Rom. 1:3-4). Two emphases are evident in this text. First, Jesus was a man, descended from David. Second, he was "designated Son of God in power . . . by his resurrection from the dead" and as such he is "Jesus Christ our Lord."

According to these texts, then, the titles "Lord" and "Messiah" or "Christ" received their full meaning (whether or not they were occasionally used earlier) in consequence of the resurrection and exaltation of Jesus. This suggestion is confirmed by much of what we read in the rest of the New Testament. At a very early point in Christian thinking the terms "Lord" and "Christ" were applied to Jesus. He was the risen and exalted Lord; he was the risen and exalted Christ. The term "Lord" is evidently very old, for it occurs in an Aramaic formula quoted by Paul in 1 Corinthians 16:22: "Marana tha!"—"our Lord, come!" Similarly "Messiah" or "Christ" is much earlier than Paul's letters, for in them he often uses the term as a proper name rather than as a title.

The implications of these terms provided a considerable stimulus to religious and even theological concern. "Messiah" was limited in its scope because it was fully comprehensible only to Jewish readers of the Old Testament, and Paul's use of it as a proper name meant that much of its earlier significance was lost. In John 20:31 the readers of the Gospel are urged to believe "that Jesus is the Christ," but the term "Christ" is then interpreted as meaning "the Son of God." On the other hand, "Lord" sounded more overtones. First, it could be understood or misunderstood by pagan hearers as meaning that Jesus could be called "Lord" as their own "many gods and many lords" (1 Cor. 8:5) could be so styled. There was a point of contact, but a dangerous one. Second, hearers who were Jews or Christians would recognize that this title was one which in their Greek Old Testament, or in their Hebrew one as it was read aloud, was regularly ascribed to God himself. This was the most important aspect of "Lord."

If Jesus was now assigned the title of God himself, how had this taken place? One answer is given in a hymn which Paul quotes (either from himself or from an earlier writer) in his letter to the Philippians (2:8–10):

He humbled himself
and became obedient unto death,
even death on a cross.
Therefore God has highly exalted him
and bestowed on him the name which is above every name,
that at the name of Jesus every knee should bow,
in heaven and on earth and under the earth,
and every tongue confess that
Jesus Christ is Lord,
to the glory of God the Father.

This part of the hymn strongly reminds us of the early ideas we have found in Acts and in Romans. God gives Jesus his own name—the name "Lord." What is new is the explanation that the reason for this ascription was the humility and obedience and death of Jesus. The most striking feature of the hymn, however, is the fact that the end of it is modeled after a passage in Isaiah (45:22–23) in which God says, "I am God, and there is none else. . . . Unto me every knee shall bow, every tongue shall swear." In the hymn Jesus is not God, but he is exceedingly close to God because God has given him his name. This idea may well have been implicit in earlier use of the title "Lord," but it was not then worked out.

Thus far only the latter half of the Philippians hymn has been quoted in order to show its links with earlier tradition. In the preceding verses, however, there is a new element in Christian thinking (Phil. 2:6–7):

Though he was in the form of God,
[he] did not count equality with God a thing to be grasped,

but emptied himself,
taking the form of a servant,
being born in the likeness of men.

Here the new idea is not that Jesus was a "servant" or "slave." He had been identified with the suffering servant of Isaiah 53 at a relatively early point in Christian thinking. What is new is that "the form of God" is differentiated from "the likeness of men" and Jesus' servanthood is set before his birth as well as after it. His obedience to God is an eternal obedience; his humility is expressed not only in his death but also in his incarnation. The word we use for such an idea is "pre-existence."

Now this idea is not necessarily philosophical. It has roots in the Hebrew prophetic idea of vocation, in conformity with God's eternal purpose. Thus the prophet Jeremiah hears the word of the Lord saying, "Before I formed thee in the belly I knew thee; and before thou camest forth out of the womb I sanctified thee, and I ordained thee a prophet unto the nations" (Jer. 1:5). Paul himself could interpret his vocation in the same way: "He who had set me apart before I was born, and had called me through his grace, was pleased to reveal his Son in me in order that I might preach him among the nations" (Gal. 1:15–16). This, we may suppose, is the origin of conceptions of pre-existence. But the Philippians passage goes beyond vocation to discuss the life of Christ with God. He was "in the form of God" presumably, as in other Pauline passages, because he was the very Image of God in relation to which man was created. Unlike Adam, or even Satan, chief of the rebellious angels, he did not grasp for equality with God (or, alternatively, did not insist upon retaining the equality he possessed), but "emptied himself" and became a human being. That of which he emptied himself was evidently what differentiates God from man, and this, as we saw in the first essay in this volume, consisted essentially of the attributes of power and imperishability. Both attributes were abandoned when he became man and was crucified. The power of God was only paradoxically present in the crucifixion (1 Cor. 1:22–25)—though it was still present, for the one whom the rulers of this age crucified was still "the Lord of glory" (1 Cor. 2:8). The imperishability of God was only paradoxically present in one who was born as a man and died as a man—though it was still present, for God raised him and exalted him.

It would appear that Christian thought proceeded from eternal vocation to eternal existence and that then it could concern itself with the nature and the purpose of pre-existence. At this point another motif of theological concern entered the picture. According to the Jewish expectations of God's reign, God was going to effect a new creation in the last days; and the apostle Paul frequently refers to this new creation as having come into existence for Christians. "If any one is in Christ, he is a new creation; the old has passed away, behold, the new has come" (2 Cor. 5:17). In this new world of resurrection after death, "the world has been crucified to me, and I to the world; neither circumcision nor uncircumcision counts for anything, but a new creation" (Gal. 6:14–15). This new creation has been brought into being by Christ. And if God's eternal purpose is realized through the new creation in Christ, this purpose must be a continuation of his original creative act, and Christ must be involved in both creations. Thus Paul combines the two events when he says, "It is the God who said, 'Let light shine out of the darkness,' who has shone in our hearts to give the light of the knowledge of the glory of God in the face of Christ" (2 Cor. 4:6).

Given, then, the instrumentality of Christ in both creations, how were the early Christians to explain his role in the original creation of the universe? Once more, they turned to the Old Testament, and there they found (as other Jews had found in their time) the mysterious personification of God's Wisdom in the Book of Proverbs—and also in Ecclesiasticus and in some of the other apocryphal literature. In the eighth chapter of Proverbs Wisdom says,

The Lord created me at the beginning of his work,
the first of his acts of old.
Ages ago I was set up,
at the first, before the beginning of the earth.
When there were no depths I was brought forth,
when there were no springs abounding with water.
Before the mountains had been shaped,
before the hills, I was brought forth;
before he had made the earth with its fields,
or the first of the dust of the world.
When he established the heavens, I was there,
when he drew a circle on the face of the deep,
when he made firm the skies above,
when he established the fountains of the deep
when he assigned to the sea its limit,
so that the waters might not transgress his command,
when he marked out the foundations of the earth,
then I was beside him, like a master workman;

and I was daily his delight,
rejoicing before him always,
rejoicing in his inhabited world
and delighting in the sons of men.

I have quoted this passage in full because of the remarkable influence it exerted upon the imagination of Jews
and Christians alike. For instance, in Ecclesiasticus
(24:3ff.) Wisdom says, "I came forth from the mouth
of the Most High and covered the earth as a mist. I
dwelt in high places, and my throne is in the pillar of
cloud. . . . The Creator of all things . . . created me
from the beginning before the world." She is evidently
God's instrument in his creation of the universe.

And she is not only the instrument of creation.
Through her is given the revelation of God. As we read
in the first-century Hellenistic-Jewish book of the Wisdom of Solomon, she is

a vapor of the power of God,
and an emanation from the pure glory of the Almighty;
therefore nothing defiled can find entrance into her.
For she is radiance from eternal light
and an unspotted mirror of the working of God
and an image of his goodness [7:25–26].

When Christians, conscious of the pre-existence of
Christ and his role both in creation and in revelation,
wanted to express their ideas more fully, they inevitably
turned to this Old Testament figure and used Wisdom
language to describe the work of Christ. In the first two
chapters of 1 Corinthians Paul contrasts a wisdom that is
merely human with the wisdom of God and identifies
Christ as God's power and wisdom. More explicitly,
when he speaks of the activities of God the Father and

the Lord Jesus Christ, in a passage to which we referred in the first essay (1 Cor. 8:6), the functions he assigns to Christ are the functions of the pre-existent Wisdom of God, the one through whom the world was made.

Most explicitly the same picture is set forth in the famous Christological hymn of Colossians 1:15–20. This hymn has two parts, the first concerning Christ's work in creation, the second concerning his work in redemption and reconciliation. The second part is based primarily on the apostolic preaching about Christ's work. The first, with which we are here concerned, sets forth Christ's agency in the creation.

He is the image of the invisible God,
    the first-born of all creation;
for in him all things were created,
      in heaven and on earth,
      visible and invisible,
    whether thrones or dominions or principalities or authorities;
      all things were created through him
                and for him.
He is before all things, and
in him all things hold together.

This part of the hymn cannot be based upon Proverbs alone, for in Proverbs, Wisdom is not God's image. It must, instead, be fashioned after the likeness of the Book of Wisdom, where Wisdom is an image of God and was present with him when he made the world (9:9). But it is also based on Proverbs, for the expression "first-born of all creation" is almost certainly based on "first of his acts of old" in Proverbs 8:22. After the declaration about the pre-existent Christ as Wisdom and image and first-born comes a detailed explanation of his functions in the work of creation. In essence, it consists of three elements: "he," meaning Christ; "all things," meaning everything apart from and inferior to Christ and the God whose image he is; and four prepositions intended to indicate the relationships between him and them. The point is that all things were created in him, through him, and for him, and that he is before them all.

A clue as to the possible origin of this explanation is provided in an expression which we have not yet quoted: "he is the beginning." For a reader of the Old Testament this expression would recall not only Proverbs 8:22 ("the Lord created me at the beginning") but also the first verse of Genesis: "in the beginning God made the heaven and the earth." We can see that literally "in the beginning" has a temporal reference. But among ancient Jews and Christians, accustomed to read the Bible rather imaginatively (or rather, literally and imaginatively at the same time), there was a feeling that the preposition "in" expressed only one of the relationships between God and his "beginning," which was his Wisdom. If "in" was appropriate, so were "through" and "for." Furthermore, these prepositions had, or could have, a deeper causal significance. "In" is usually instrumental; it can therefore be replaced by "through." But if Christ or Wisdom is the instrument through which God worked, and he or she is also the image of God, he or she can also be regarded as the final cause or goal of the creation, and therefore "for" can be substituted for "in."

We need not linger over the visible and invisible "thrones, dominions, principalities, and authorities." The reason they are mentioned is that the author simply wants to set forth the total range of the work of God's creation through Christ,[3] and to show that nothing was created by any other means; all God's creation is good and came into existence through him. This is to say that Christ represents not just the "religious" purpose of God; he reflects God's purpose in its entirety.

The unknown author of the letter to the Hebrews makes the same point in a similar way and relies on the same kinds of ideas. "In many and various ways God spoke of old to our fathers by the prophets; but in these last days he has spoken to us by a Son, whom he appointed to be the heir of all things, through whom also be created the world. He reflects the glory of God and bears the very stamp of his nature, upholding the universe by his word of power" (Heb. 1:1–3). Once more revelation and creation are bound together, and the language about reflecting God's glory and bearing the stamp of his nature is almost certainly derived from Wisdom 7:25–26. In the last days, in which Christians live, the agent of creation became the agent of final revelation and made God's eternal purpose known to them.

In the New Testament, however, the cardinal text related to our subject is to be found in the opening verses of the Gospel of John. It is sometimes supposed that in the prologue to this Gospel (John 1:1–18) we can find traces of an old Gnostic hymn, not really related to Christ at all but appropriated and worked over by Christians. From what we have already seen of Chris-

---

[3] Origen (De princ. 1, 7, 1 [p. 86 Koetschau]) notes that "visible and invisible" provides a general statement, while "thrones," etc., supply specific examples.

tian thought, however, it is obvious that we have no need of such a hypothesis. The author of the Gospel is almost certainly using material distinct from the rest of his book, with which he links it by comments about John the Baptist (1:6–8, 15; continuing with 1:19ff.). But there is no reason to suppose that the evangelist did not write the prologue himself or that it was not he who combined the prologue with the Gospel.

For the moment we are concerned with only the first three verses.

> In the beginning was the Word,
> and the Word was with God,
> and the Word was God.
> He was in the beginning with God;
> and all things were made through him,
> and without him was not anything made that was made.

The Greek for "word" is *logos*, and scholars have often been fascinated by the fact that this term occurs in the fragments of Heraclitus, among the Stoics, and—as analogous to God's creative Wisdom—in the writings of Philo of Alexandria. There is little to suggest that John had read anything about these philosophers, although the influence of Philo *may* have reached the circles in which he wrote. It seems more probable that like the other Christians we have discussed he read the Old Testament. From the book of Genesis he knew that the universe was created by God's word; God spoke and the creation came into existence. And like the other Christian writers he correlated God's act of revelation with his act of creation. It was God's word which came to the prophets; it was God's word which was finally expressed in his Son; and the word of creation was the same word as the word of revelation.

The possible background of John's thought should not have been discussed before what he says was considered, but it seemed advisable to do so because often so much emphasis has been placed on the background—at the expense of the text itself. What the text says is very clear. John first makes three statements about the Word, explaining, as Origen says, "in whom," "in relation to whom," and "who" the Word was.[4] The Word was in the beginning, with God, and God. The first expression is primarily temporal, although as we have already seen such expressions could also suggest that the "beginning" was either Wisdom or Christ or, as in this instance, God himself. What John is emphasizing is the eternal pre-existence of the Word in association with God, as well as the belief that one who does so eternally pre-exist actually *is* God. Origen had considerable difficulty with this expression. Like Philo, he differentiated the Greek expression ὁ θεός (God, with the definite article) from θεός (God, without the article) and he claimed that in the Bible only the former expression was employed in regard to God the Father.[5] This distinction does not seem to be present in John's mind. He has already differentiated the Word from God by saying that the Word was with God; now he goes on to say that the Word *was* God.[6] For him there is

---

[4] *Ioh. comm.* 2, 4 (p. 57 Preuschen).

[5] Philo, *Somn.* 1, 229–30; Origen, *Ioh. comm.* 2, 2 (p. 54 Preuschen).

[6] For the translation as "God" cf. E. C. Colwell in *Journal of Biblical Literature* 52 (1933), 12–21.

only one God, and the pre-existent Word can be identified with this God just as the incarnate Christ could say, "The Father and I are one" (John 10:30). This is not to say that "God was the Word." The identity is one which the later fathers called one of substance, and one cannot reverse the terms without distorting John's meaning. In the mystery of creation and revelation the Father and the Son are both one and distinct. The Father is also greater than the Son (John 14:28).

The last verses quoted reiterate the distinctiveness of the Word ("this one was in the beginning with God") and go on to set forth the totality of the creative act which took place through him. Positively, everything was made through him; negatively, nothing was made apart from him. The same point has been expressed in Colossians.

What is this prologue about? In John's time among philosophers and non-philosophers as well there was an urgent concern about the nature of the universe. The problem was essentially whether the world was God's or belonged to his adversaries, for the idea that it came from a fortuitous concourse of atoms was maintained only by a tiny minority. Nearly every philosophical school tried to make sense of the *Timaeus* of Plato, which provides a mythological description of how a "demiurge" or fashioner of pre-existent matter shaped the universe. Philo of Alexandria reworked this description, apparently maintaining that God made the matter himself. For Jews and Christians the fundamental source of knowledge was the biblical revelation, and there, in the book of Genesis, we find creation described. John has what we may call an existential concern with Genesis. He believes that the authentic clue to the meaning of creation has been revealed in Jesus of Nazareth, who, as he knows from Christian tradition, is the pre-existent Word and Son of God. Since Jesus came from God to give light and life to men, he obviously manifested God's original purpose of giving light and life; the light and life at the end can be no different from the light and life at the beginning. In the beginning—so Genesis begins—what was there? or rather, *who* was there? In the beginning was the creative and revelatory Word which God spoke, bringing light out of darkness, saying, "Let there be light." Such a creative Word could be neither less than God, since God the Creator spoke it from himself, nor more than God, since he is the sole Creator, and it was his Word which he spoke. Since it was the Word of the Creator, nothing was made separately from it.

John is concerned not only with the pre-existent work of the Word but also with the mystery of his incarnation in Jesus. Apart from the self-revelation of the incarnate Word we should be confronted with little more than the speculations of Plato or Philo. Creation provides the indispensable preface to revelation and redemption, but it is only the preface. The climax of the prologue is reached in the eighteenth verse: "and the Word became flesh and tabernacled among us, and we beheld his glory." Every word counts here. "Flesh" is used in many senses in the New Testament, and for John himself it is usually contrasted with "spirit." It has potentially unfavorable connotations. Here, however, the Word himself *becomes* flesh. The creative power of

God comes to be present in a human being in such a way that by the intuitive grasp of faith one can recognize the glory or presence of God; one can see in Jesus the manifestation of God's eternal purpose. Once more we ask how John could have said this in regard to Jesus of Nazareth.

The clue to the sentence seems to be given chiefly by the word which is translated "tabernacled." It can mean no more than "dwelt," but in view of its supremely important position in what John is saying, I venture to assign it a more special reference. The Greek word is *eskēnōsen;* I propose to treat it as equivalent to the compound form *kataskēnoun,* which the Greek translators of the Old Testament preferred.[7]

Now if we look at the Greek Old Testament to see who or what was expected to "tabernacle" or "be enshrined" in the world, especially among the people of God, we seem to find clear clues to John's understanding of the incarnation. Since we have already found Wisdom themes in Christological thought, we are not surprised to notice that in Ecclesiasticus 24:8 Wisdom says, "The Creator gave a resting-place to my tabernacle and said, 'Tabernacle in Jacob.' " But John never explicitly mentions the Wisdom of God. More important for him is the conception of the "name" of God, another Jewish expression for God's presence in the world and among men. We see that this is so when we look at the prayer of John 17: "I have manifested thy name"; "Keep them in thy name which thou hast given me"; "I made known to them thy name." It is therefore significant that according to several of the Old

[7] For this equivalence see Ps. 25(26):8 and Rev. 21:3.

Testament prophets God has declared that he once made his name be tabernacled in Shiloh (and by inference in Jerusalem, Jer. 7:12) and that he will make it be tabernacled "in the midst of the house of Israel forever" (Ezek. 43:7; cf. 2 Esd. 11:9 = Neh. 1:9).[8] But to say that God's name tabernacles among men is also to say that God himself tabernacles among men, and this is what we clearly find in a Psalm (67[68 Hebrew]:17), in Ezekiel 43:9, and above all in Zechariah.[9]

Sing and rejoice, O daughter of Zion;
for lo, I come and I will tabernacle in your midst [2:10].
I will tabernacle in the midst of Jerusalem,
and Jerusalem will be called the true city,
and the mountain of the Lord Almighty, the holy mount [8:3].
I will tablernacle in the midst of Jerusalem,
and I will be their God in truth and righteousness [8:8].

God's presence obviously involves his glory, which means not only his radiance but also his might. On Mount Sinai "the tabernacle was filled with the glory of the Lord" (Ex. 40:34–35); so a psalmist could declare, "Lord, I have loved the beauty of thy house and the place of the tabernacling of thy glory" (Ps. 25[26]:8).[10]

Themes of this kind were combined in John's mind as he tried to express the meaning of God's Word becom-

---

[8] God's Name is also to be in his messenger who will lead the people into the land of promise (Exod. 23:21).

[9] Cf. Melito, *Pasch. hom.* (p. 7, 25 Bonner; lines 258–59 Lohse).

[10] It may be added that this background probably explains John's insistence that the older Jewish sacrificial system and the temple itself had been replaced by Jesus, God's true tabernacle; cf. John 1:29; 2:6–11; 2:15–16; 2:21; 4:20–24.

ing flesh, just as in an early Christian prayer which we find in the *Didache* (late first century) we encounter them again:

We give thee thanks, holy Father,
for thy holy Name
which thou didst make tabernacle in our hearts,
and for the knowledge and faith and immortality
which thou didst make known to us through thy servant
    Jesus:
to thee be glory forever [*Did.* 11:2].

The difference between John and the Didachist lies in the fact that the former is more of a theologian; he has worked out more of the implications of his ideas. We refer to the *Didache* simply to show that the motifs were present in Christian circles even when the implications were not worked out.

How was it possible for John to make such statements about Jesus? How could he represent Thomas as saying to the risen Saviour, "My Lord and my God" (John 20:28)? The fact that he is expressing a common faith, as we have seen when we traced the earlier use of similar expressions among Christians, does not necessarily convince us that we ought to share it. For modern men tradition does not cut much ice; we like to hear about first-hand, verifiable experience. It seems to me that John is reporting such experience. At the end of his book he tells us what his purpose is: he has written "so that you may believe that Jesus if the Christ, the Son of God, and that by believing you may have life in his name" (20:31). We may not be too far wrong if we regard many of the stories and sayings in the book as reflections of the evangelist's experience. He feels that he has passed from death to life; he feels that the Lamb of God has taken away his sin; he feels that he has beheld the glory of God's light, that he has experienced judgment and resurrection, that he has been born again, that he has been given eternal life. He is writing a gospel, not a letter, but there is little difference between what he says and what Paul writes more personally: "I have been crucified with Christ; it is no longer I who live, but Christ who lives in me; and the life I now live in the flesh I live by faith in the Son of God, who loved me and gave himself for me" (Gal. 2:20).

By meditating on the story of Jesus and by appropriating it as an archetype of his own experience, John has come to know what he regards as the purpose of God in revelation and redemption. If it is God's purpose now, it has always been God's purpose—at creation and in creation. The glory of God which Jesus manifested was the glory which was his "before the foundation of the world" (John 17:24); it was this glory which the prophet Isaiah beheld (12:41). In the beginning was God's purpose, and this purpose was revealed in a historical encounter which gave new direction to the disciples of Jesus. Jesus loved his disciples, and they loved him because they were in harmony with the eternal love of God for the world (John 3:16). To be sure, men crucified God's incarnate purpose, but God's love and his power were not overcome; in this crucifixion lay the exaltation of his purpose. His purpose was lifted up so that it could be seen by all and could be followed by all. The crucifixion was exaltation because, from the Christian point of view, the only way to gain one's life is to lose it. For John the losing is the gaining.

Jesus is "the way, the truth, and the life" (14:6).

The meaning of John's doctrine, then, is that God's eternal purpose, the mysterious clue to the understanding of human history and individual existence, was manifest in Jesus of Nazareth. To be sure, "purpose" may not be the best translation for "word." Goethe preferred "deed." But it at least implies that there is a direction to human existence, known by faith to those who accept Jesus as its expression, and that this direction is not arbitrary or based simply on a nostalgic enthusiasm for Jesus as a teacher. Among some modern theologians there is such a nostalgic enthusiasm. But just as the apostle Paul had to say that "what we preach is not ourselves, but Jesus Christ as Lord, with ourselves as your servants for Jesus' sake" (2 Cor. 4:5), and could also say that "as men of sincerity, as commissioned by God, in the sight of God we speak in Christ" (2 Cor. 2:17), so also Jesus did not proclaim himself as himself but spoke and acted in obedience to the will of God his Father. This is to say, if we continue to use the word "purpose," that he made God's purpose his purpose. He preached not himself but God his Father, with himself as God's servant for God's sake. We cannot accept literally the poetic language of the apostles about Christ's function in the creation of the world; we can try, however, to reinterpret it in ways analogous to the intentions of the apostles. One of the most important points we must maintain is the idea that Jesus was not speaking arbitrarily or completely *de novo*. He was revealing what could be understood, or half-understood, about man's existence in relation to God—something which is not conditioned by circumstances or changed in various historical environments, whether or not men live in accordance with it. This something is that authentic human existence is to be found in the love of God and expressed in the love of our fellow men.

This is why when John comes to describe Christ's last supper with his disciples he not only shares Luke's insistence upon servanthood as a lesson of primary importance (Luke 22:24–27; John 13:3–16) but also represents Jesus as saying, "A new commandment I give to you, that you love one another; even as I have loved you, that you also love one another" (John 13:34). But as is pointed out in the first letter of John, the commandment of love is not only new because of its setting in the new age; it is also old and "from the beginning" (2:7–8; 3:11). It is not arbitrary; it is founded on the primeval creative love which God bears toward his creation (John 3:16)—the God who himself is love (1 John 4:8).

At this point, I believe, we have reached the climax of the New Testament presentation of Christ in relation to God: Christ is the revealer and the representer of God's love for the world, a love which man is bound to reciprocate in gratitude or (more explicitly) to share with others. "In this is love, not that we loved God but that he loved us. . . . If God so loved us, we ought to love one another; if we love one another, God abides in us and his love is perfected in us" (1 John 4:10–12).

In the postapostolic church this insight was expressed rather less frequently than we should expect. Perhaps this was true because much of the surviving literature is concerned with practical and doctrinal conflict. It may also have been true because it was easier to discuss God in the various ways we mentioned in the first lecture than to introduce the idea that he is love. Few early theologians really took love seriously, as far as we can tell from their writings. Notable exceptions are provided by Ignatius of Antioch and by Origen, although, as Bishop Nygren has pointed out in regard to Origen, the love motif is mixed with other motifs and to some extent watered down.[11] As the doctrine of the Trinity was worked out, the conception of God as love played little part in it until we reach Augustine's famous interpretation of God as the one who loves, the Son as the one who is loved, and the Spirit as the love that binds them together. This idea arises in Christian circles rather late, however, and the Christological statements of the second century generally treat Christ not as the expression of God's love but as the "reason" of God's mind. In them the Johannine term *logos* is now interpreted in relation to Stoic and Middle Platonic philosophy and, finally, to the thought of Philo of Alexandria. In Middle Platonism a model was provided for viewing the supreme God as indescribable and the Second God as the fashioner of the universe. It would appear that Justin, for example, used a pattern like this.

In the late second century Christological ideas were expressed not only in philosophical terms but also in vivid sermonic rhetoric. Conspicuous examples come from the paschal sermon by Melito of Sardis, first published in 1940 and more recently found in another Greek papyrus and in Coptic. Melito and his hearers delighted in brief, sloganlike expressions, which are

[11] *Agape and Eros* (rev. trans.; London, 1953), 387–92; on Ignatius, 261.

characteristic of Asianic rhetoric but are none the less theological.[12] Christ

> was buried as man,
> was raised from the dead as God,
> being by nature both God and man.
> He is all things.
> In that he judges, law;
> in that he teaches, word;
> in that he saves, grace;
> in that he begets, Father;
> in that he is begotten, Son;
> in that he suffers, sheep;
> in that he is buried, man;
> in that he rises, God.[13]

Most of these expressions are concerned with the paradoxical mystery of the incarnation. At the end of the sermon, however, Melito uses the same style in order to set forth a more complete picture of Christ before the incarnation, during it, and afterward. It is he

> who made new the heaven and the earth,
> who in the beginning fashioned man,
> who is proclaimed through law and prophets,
> who was made flesh in the virgin,
> who was hanged on a tree,
> who was buried in the earth,
> who was raised again from the dead,
> and ascended to the heights of the heavens,
> and sat down at the right hand of the Father,
> to whom be glory for ever and ever. Amen.[14]

[12] For this point see my article on "Scripture, Rhetoric and Theology in Theophilus," in *Vigiliae Christianae* 13 (1959), 33–45.

[13] Lines 47–57 Lohse (sections 8–9 Bonner); the Bodmer text is practically identical with this. For references see p. 94, note 34.

[14] Lines 707–16 Lohse (section 104 Bonner).

Instead of giving the doxology at this point, the Bodmer text continues:

who has authority to judge all, to save,
through whom the Father created from the beginning
    forever.
He is the Alpha and the Omega,
he is the beginning and end;
inexpressible beginning and inconceivable end;
he is the Christ,
he is the King,
he is Jesus;
he is commander,
he is the Lord,
he is the one who rose from the dead,
he is the one who sits at the right hand of the Father.
He bears the Father and is borne by the Father,
to whom be glory and might forever. Amen.

It is the religious feeling, here expressed in rhetoric, for the supreme meaningfulness of Christ in relation to human existence and to the universe in which human existence is set that has produced the development of Christological doctrine. We may not be as fond of rhetoric as Melito was. We must recognize, however, that underneath it lies a passionate recognition of what Christ meant to him, to the Christian community, and to the world.

This recognition was certainly shared by one of Melito's contemporaries, an unorthodox theologian named Apelles. In his old age Apelles grew weary of theological debate and when the question of the "first principle" came up once more he said, "We need not investigate this matter at all; each one should remain in his original conviction. For those who have set their hope on the Crucified will be saved, if only they are found in good works. To me the most obscure question of all is that concerning God, though there is one first principle." In response to further argument he replied, "I do not *know* how there is one first principle, but I *am moved* in this direction; I do not *understand* how the uncreated God is one, but this I *believe*."[15]

The great Ritschlian church historian Harnack found this confession wholly admirable. It is based on Pauline language: salvation by hope, the Crucified, "to be found in," even good works.[16] It is also obviously antimetaphysical. In Harnack's view Apelles rightly recognized the superiority of saving faith to philosophical theology.

Unfortunately, when philosophical theology is driven out the door, it has a way of coming back through the window. We know that while for Apelles there was indeed one first principle, the good God, there were also three or four more secondary divinities whom he called "angels." There was the creator, merely just, who made the universe and may have been identical with the "fiery" angel who spoke to Moses.[17] There was also an angel who was the source of evil; and there was the Crucified, who came from the first principle and returned to him. As the antiheretical Roman writer Hip-

[15] Eusebius, *Historia ecclesiastica* 5, 13, 5–6; cf. A. von Harnack, *Marcion: Das Evangelium von fremden Gott* (*Texte und Untersuchungen* 45; Leipzig, 1924), 177–96; 404*–20*.

[16] Salvation by hope: Rom. 8:24, 1 Cor. 15:19, 2 Cor. 1:10; the Crucified: 1 Cor. 1:23, 2:2; "to be found in": Phil. 3:9; good works: 2 Cor. 5:10, etc. (Harnack, *op. cit.*, 182).

[17] Deut. 4:24; Exod. 24:17. For the identification cf. J. H. Waszink, *Tertullian De anima* (Amsterdam, 1947), 300.

polytus pointed out, Apelles actually ended up with five powers, not one.[18]

This is hardly the simple piety which Harnack lauded. Like his teacher Marcion, Apelles made use of Pauline language and ideas, but he did so in a context which was ultimately Gnostic rather than Christian. Both Apelles and his teacher Marcion vigorously rejected the Old Testament with its revelation of God as the good creator of a good world. In this respect they were hardly faithful to the teaching of Paul. Their supreme God, they believed, was the one whom Jesus addressed as Father, but they depicted both the Father and Jesus as totally alien from the world and from mankind.

The doctrine of the Trinity, to which I shall turn in the next essay, is closer, it seems to me, to the experience of the Christian community and to the teaching of the apostles than is that of Apelles. Harnack's defense of him has been mentioned in support of the view that an apparently simple devotion to Jesus may often involve surprising presuppositions or implications. Any "historical Jesus" who can be discovered by historical research is historically incomprehensible apart from his conviction that he was obeying the living God and was calling others to a like obedience. This, as I have suggested, lies at the foundation of the Christian doctrine of the Incarnation.

This is not to say that the early church adequately and permanently solved all the problems related to the nature of the Son of God. In a papyrus published in 1949 we possess a fascinating account of a "discussion of

[18] Hippolytus, *Ref.* 7, 38, 1 (p. 224 Wendland); 10, 20, 1 (p. 280).

Origen with Heraclides and the bishops with him, concerning the Father, the Son, and the soul."[19] A translation of the opening pages of this discussion is given here because it carries us into the kind of arena in which early patristic theological questions were often fought out.

Since the bishops present had raised questions about the faith of the bishop Heraclides, so that in the presence of all he might acknowledge his faith, and each of them had made remarks and had raised the question, the bishop Heraclides said: "And I too believe exactly what the divine scriptures say: 'In the beginning was the Word, and the Word was with God, and the Word was God. He was in the beginning with God. All things came into existence through him, and nothing came into existence apart from him.' So we agree in the faith and, furthermore, we believe that the Christ assumed flesh, that he was born, that he ascended into the heavens with the flesh in which he arose, and that he is seated at the right hand of the Father, whence he is going to come and judge the living and the dead, being God and man."

Origen said: "Since a debate is now beginning and one may speak on the subject of the debate, I will speak. The whole church is here to listen. One church should not differ from another in knowledge, since you are not the false community. I ask you, Father Heraclides. God is the almighty, the uncreated, the supreme one who made all things. Do you agree?"

Heraclides said: "I agree; for thus I too believe."

Origen said: "Christ Jesus, who exists in the form of God, though he is distinct from God in the form in which he existed, was he God before he entered a body or not?"

Heraclides said: "He was God before."

[19] J. Scherer, *Entretien d'Origène avec Héraclide et les évêques ses collègues sur le Père, le Fils, et l'âme* (*Publications de la Société Fouad I de Papyrologie, Textes et Documents*, IX; Cairo, 1949).

Origen said: "He was God before he entered a body, or not?"

Heraclides said: "Yes."

Origen said: "God distinct from this God in whose form he existed?"

Heraclides said: "Obviously distinct from any other, since he is in the form of that one who created everything."

Origen said: "Was there not a God, Son of God, the only-begotten of God, the first-born of all creation, and do we not devoutly say that in one sense there are two Gods and, in another, one God?"

Heraclides said: "What you say is clear; but we say that there is God, the almighty, without beginning and without end, containing all things but not contained, and there is his Word, Son of the living God, God and man, through whom all things came into existence, God in relation to the Spirit and man in that he was born of Mary."

Origen said: "You do not seem to have answered my question. Make it clear; perhaps I did not follow you. Is the Father God?"

Heraclides said: "Certainly."

Origen said: "Is the Son distinct from the Father?"

Heraclides said: "How can he be Son if he is also Father?"

Origen said: "While distinct from the Father, is the Son himself also God?"

Heraclides said: "He himself is also God."

Origen said: "And the two Gods become one?"

Heraclides said: "Yes."

Origen said: "Do we acknowledge two Gods?"

Heraclides said: "Yes; the power is one."

Origen said: "But since our brethren are shocked by the affirmation that there are two Gods, the subject must be examined with care in order to show in what respect they are two and in what respect the two are one God."

Origen then proceeded to argue from scripture and from the prayers of Christians that the "dyad" and the "henad" must be preserved at the same time, without falling into the illusion that there is a single source of deity (*monarchia*) or denying the deity of Christ. It proved easier to identify these errors than to avoid them, as we shall see when we come to deal with trinitarian doctrine. Like the early Christian doctrine about the Father, the doctrine of the Son cannot ultimately be resolved without recourse to paradox. At the same time, the early Christian theologians were willing to employ rational arguments as far as they could, without doing violence to the underlying religious realities on which their philosophical theology was based.

III

THE HOLY SPIRIT AND THE TRINITY

WE MIGHT suppose that when we have spoken of God the Father and of his Son Jesus Christ we have said all that needs saying about the early Christian doctrine of God. Certainly in the primitive credal formula of 1 Corinthians 8:6, to which I have referred several times, there is no mention of anything but the one God, the Father and the one Lord, Jesus Christ; and the same point can be made in regard to the Christological hymns in Philippians and Colossians. It is obvious, nevertheless, that mention of the Father and the Son came to be regarded as somehow incomplete unless there was also mention of the Holy Spirit. At the end of the Gospel of Matthew we learn that the risen Lord commanded his

disciples to "go and make disciples of all nations, baptiz-
ing them in the name of the Father and of the Son and
of the Holy Spirit" (28:19). We must therefore inquire
who the Holy Spirit is.

Perhaps the best point at which to begin occurs in
Paul's letter to the Romans. In the sixth and seventh
chapters he has been discussing the human situation.
Though redeemed by Christ, man is still double-
minded, since sin still dwells within him. Is there any
solution for his problem? Yes, says Paul, there is. "To
set the mind on the flesh is death, but to set the mind on
the Spirit is life and peace" (Rom. 8:6). And in
Romans 8:9–12 he tries to explain why this is so.

You are not in the flesh, you are in the Spirit, if the Spirit of
God really dwells in you. Any one who does not have the
Spirit of Christ does not belong to him. But if Christ is in you,
although your bodies are dead because of sin, your spirits are
alive because of righteousness. If the Spirit of him who raised
Jesus from the dead dwells in you, he who raised Christ Jesus
from the dead will give life to your mortal bodies also through
his Spirit which dwells in you.

This passage clearly indicates that for Paul the functions
of "the Spirit of God," "the Spirit of Christ," and the
risen Christ are identical. There is a strict parallelism
among these functions, and Paul does not differentiate
one from another. He does differentiate God the Father
both from Christ and from the Spirit of God or Christ,
even though in 1 Corinthians 14:24 he says that an
outsider who hears Christians prophesying through the
Spirit will declare that God is really among them.
Where the Spirit of the Lord is, there is freedom (2
Cor. 3:17), and, one may add, there is God. But just as

in the Gospel of John we read that the Word was God, though God in his fulness was not the Word, so here we should say that while the Spirit is God, God in his fulness is not the Spirit. The Spirit is the Spirit *of* God.

But what is the Spirit? Above all, it would appear, the Spirit is the agent through which God brings the Christian community into existence and gives gifts to it.

No one can say "Jesus is Lord" except by the Holy Spirit. Now there are varieties of gifts, but the same Spirit; and there are varieties of service, but the same Lord; and there are varieties of working, but it is the same God who inspires them all in every one. To each is given the manifestation of the Spirit for the common good [1 Cor. 12:3–7].

Once more we encounter the identity of functions among the Spirit, the Lord, and God himself,[1] but when Paul speaks of the life of Christians in the community he tends to speak primarily of the work of the Spirit. "By one Spirit we were all baptized into one body—Jews or Greeks, slaves or free—and all were made to drink of one Spirit" (1 Cor. 12:13). The Spirit produces fruits in Christians, fruits which take the place of obedience to the old law and at the same time transcend it. "The fruit of the Spirit is love, joy, peace, patience, kindness, goodness, faithfulness, gentleness, self-control" (Gal. 5:22–23).

What we have been describing reflects Paul's great contributions to the doctrine of the Spirit. Before his time, as well as in some of the communities he founded, there were those who seemed to regard the Spirit simply as a power which produced increased vitality and exu-

[1] Compare also 2 Cor. 13:13, Gal. 4:4, 6, Eph. 4:4–6, and 1 Pet. 1:2.

berance among them. According to Acts 2:13 some of those at Jerusalem who observed how the Holy Spirit filled the apostles at Pentecost mockingly suggested that they were full of new wine. In his reply Peter argued that this was not the case because it was only the third hour of the day (2:15). At Corinth there were Christians who were accustomed to talk in tongues, to utter unintelligible words in the Spirit. In writing to them Paul states that he can speak in tongues more than any of them, but that he would rather speak five words with his mind, so as to instruct others, than ten thousand words in a tongue (1 Cor. 14:18–19). He may imply that some of his converts brought talking in tongues with them from paganism (1 Cor. 12:2–3); he criticizes the practice not on the ground that it is pagan but on the ground that it is often unintelligent, unintelligible, and unedifying. A conception of the Spirit as the source of rather indiscriminate vitality seems to lie in the background of Paul's reinterpretation or fresh emphasis. This is not to say that he rejects the vital religious power expressed in the new life of the believer: "Do not quench the Spirit," he writes; "do not despise prophesying." These words he wrote to the Thessalonians (1 Thess. 5:19–20) at a time when he was actually at Corinth. But he did add one more counsel: "Test everything; hold fast to what is good, abstain from every form of evil." For him "good and evil" stand above undifferentiated vitality.

We have already seen that for Paul the work of the Spirit is co-ordinate with the work of God and of Christ. In his letters he has very little to say about the life of Jesus of Nazareth, even though he certainly knew a good deal about it (1 Cor. 11:23). As he says, "even though we once regarded Christ from a human point of view, we regard him thus no longer" (2 Cor. 5:16). The problem of the relationship between Jesus and the Spirit therefore did not concern him. This problem is faced in the gospels, especially in the Gospel of John. In part it seems to have been made difficult by the fact that so little of Jesus' teaching was concerned with the Spirit. In the several gospels the Spirit is mentioned chiefly in relation to Jesus' baptism and birth. After his baptism by John, he sees the heavens opened and the Spirit descending upon him like a dove (Mark 1:10 and parallels); when John tells the story he does not mention Jesus' baptism by John but lays all his emphasis on John's witness to the descent of the Spirit (John 1:29–34). The story is evidently told to explain how it was that Jesus began his ministry, whether or not it goes back to Jesus himself. Again, in both Matthew and Luke it is made clear that the Spirit was involved in Jesus' conception. Just as God had visited Abraham's wife Sarah (Gen. 21:1), had answered the prayer of Isaac for Rebekah (Gen. 25:21), and had made Jacob's wives Leah and Rachel conceive (Gen. 29:31; 30:22) —though human parentage was also involved in these cases, as in that of the birth of Cain (Gen. 4:1)—so now Mary was "with child of the Holy Spirit" (Matt. 1:18); the angel Gabriel had said to her, "The Holy Spirit will come upon you, and the power of the Most High will overshadow you" (Luke 1:35). In the Gospel of Matthew (1:22–23), though not elsewhere in the New Testament, the event is described as the fulfillment of the prophecy of Isaiah 7:14: "Behold, a virgin shall conceive and bear a son, and his name shall be called Emmanu-el."

For Paul (as we have seen) and for John what we may call the history of the Spirit was much less significant than its actuality. Thus John can write (7:39) that a word of Jesus was enigmatically spoken "about the Spirit, which those who believed in him were to receive; for as yet the Spirit had not been given, because Jesus was not yet glorified." Indeed, John relates (16:7) that unless Jesus went away the Counselor (by which he means the Spirit, 14:25) would not come to the community of disciples; if Jesus goes away he will send the Spirit to his followers. This is to say with Paul that the Holy Spirit is the Spirit of Christ. And at the end of the Gospel the risen Jesus breathes upon the disciples (as God breathed the breath of life into man, Gen. 2:7), and imparts the Holy Spirit to them (20:22).

We have reached the point at which it would almost appear that the history of God's work of creation and redemption can be divided into periods of time. At the beginning, and in the history of Israel, came the work of the Father; during the incarnation the work of the Son was effected; and the power of God expressed in the Christian community is now the Holy Spirit. Ideas like this have occasionally been set forth by Christian theologians, perhaps most notably by Joachim de Fiore in the twelfth century. There are several difficulties with a notion of this sort, however. What is one to make of the insight that God's purpose is eternal, not expressed consecutively or (should we say) spasmodically? What of the coming of the Word of God or the Spirit of God to the Old Testament prophets? What of the mysterious statement in the second verse of Genesis to the effect that "the Spirit of God was moving over the face of the waters"?[2] A schematic periodization would be very neat but it would suggest that the ways of God and the revelation of God are more fully comprehensible than is actually the case. It would suggest that one can divide God up and put him into historical boxes. If the Christian Bible consisted only of the New Testament, we might be able to say that the Spirit revealed itself simply in the Christian community. The Old Testament reminds us that the Spirit is found outside the church and is not in the possession of the church. I have seen a confirmation certificate which states that "by the laying on of our hands we did administer Confirmation wherein were conveyed the sevenfold gifts of the Holy Spirit." This is a little too precise, even though the intention is of the best.

It would be better to say that beneath, above, in, and beyond all existence there is God, and that somehow we encounter him not only as Father but also as Son (thus the term Father is deliteralized) and as Spirit. To encounter the Father is to encounter God; to encounter the Son is to encounter God; to encounter the Spirit is to encounter God. This sounds rather mystical, and to my mind the trouble with mysticism lies in the possible implication that somehow in it we transcend our human limitations and "know God." The apostle Paul can speak of knowing God, but he usually corrects his expression by saying "or rather, being known by him" (Gal. 4:9; 1 Cor. 13:12). It would be better to say that

[2] Cf. K. Smoroński in *Biblica* 6 (1925), 140–56, 275–93, 361–95.

it is God who reveals himself to our limited apprehension as Father, Son, and Spirit.

Before we turned to our brief discussion of the Holy Spirit, we had already mentioned the baptismal formula in Matthew 28:19, with its naming of Father, Son, and Holy Spirit. During the rest of our discussion we shall be concerned with the ways in which early Christians endeavored to express the relationships among these three. Since we are dealing historically with the development of doctrine, we must make a distinction. When the Three are presented as three without any analysis of their interrelations, we shall use the term Triad, even though in Greek the word *trias* comes to mean Trinity as well. We shall reserve the term Trinity for attempts to set forth the idea that the Triad is also One, or that the Unity of God involves a Triad as well.[3]

The same formula as in the Gospel of Matthew recurs, toward the end of the first century, in the liturgical manual called the *Didache* (7, 1 and 3), but no attempt is made to explain what it means. Ignatius of Antioch mentions the Triad only twice, and each time it is fairly clear that the Father and the Son mean more to him than the Spirit does. In the first instance (*Eph.* 9, 1) he speaks of a temple and identifies it with God the Father, and of a crane of Jesus Christ, lifting stones into the temple; this crane is the cross. Almost as an afterthought

[3] W. G. Kümmel (in H. Lietzmann, *An die Korinther I–II* [Tübingen, 1949], 214) says that since the early Christian proclamation was concerned with God's eschatological act in Christ and through the Holy Spirit such a passage as II Corinthians 13:13 cannot be regarded as an anticipation of a trinitarian confession. This statement neglects the continuity between the apostolic church and what followed it.

he suggests that the rope attached to the crane is the Holy Spirit. In the second instance (*Magnesians* 13, 1) he speaks of unity "in flesh and spirit, in faith and love, in Son and Father and in Spirit, in beginning and end." All the other items are double in nature; usually he speaks only of the Father and the Son; here he mentions the Spirit only in passing. Because of the intense God mysticism and Christ mysticism which his letters reflect, there is little room for the Spirit in his thought.

At the end of the first century, however, we find clear references to the Triad. They occur in the letter written by Clement of Rome to the Corinthian church, and the fact that they are expressed almost in passing shows two things: first, there is no developed doctrine of the Trinity, and, second, the pre-eminence of the Triad is taken for granted. One reference is found in a series of rhetorical questions which obviously implies a positive answer. "Do we not have one God, and one Christ, and one Spirit of grace which has been poured out upon us?" (46:6). The other is much the same. It is present in an Old Testament kind of oath which Clement takes: "As God lives, and as the Lord Jesus Christ lives, and the Holy Spirit." These passages show that the ingredients—shall we say, "data"—for the doctrine of the Trinity continue to be present, even though the problems related to them have not been raised as yet.

The same rather naïve presentation of the Triad meets us again, half a century later, in the *First Apology* of Justin Martyr, who like Clement wrote at Rome. Responding to the pagan charge that Christians were atheists, he said that on the contrary they worshiped "the most true God, Father of righteousness and temperance and the other virtues, unrelated to wickedness," and "the Son who came from him and taught us these matters, and the army of the other good angels who follow and are like him, and the prophetic Spirit" (6, 1–2). This passage presents us with considerable difficulties. The word "other," used in relation to the angels, suggests that Jesus himself is an angel, and the place of the angels between the Son and the Spirit—as objects of worship—shows that at Rome in Justin's time there were unsolved problems in relation both to Christology and to the doctrine of angels. The popular *Shepherd* of Hermas, also from Rome and written in the generation before Justin, gives us the background of these problems, for in it there is much emphasis on angels and Christ is depicted as one of them. Justin has been unable to break free from this kind of popular theology.

We should mention that most of what Justin has to say about the Triad occurs in liturgical passages. When he speaks of Christian baptism he explains that it takes place in the name of the Father-God (though his name is really ineffable), in the name of Jesus Christ, who was crucified under Pontius Pilate, and in the name of the Holy Spirit, who through the prophets foretold the whole story of Jesus (*Apol.* 61, 10–13). Similarly at the Eucharist, Christians offer praise and glory to "the Father of all things through the name of the Son and of the Holy Spirit" (65, 3). Evidently there is a rather stable liturgical tradition in which the Triad is mentioned, although the relations of the three persons are not worked out. The beginnings of such working-out are reflected in the offering of praise and glory *to* the Father *through* Son and Spirit.

A generation after Justin we find the apologist Athenagoras seeming to straighten out Justin's language about the Triad and the angels. Athenagoras carefully states that the Triad consists of Father, Son, and Holy Spirit, and says that in addition Christians "speak of"— not worship—a multitude of angels and ministers to whom God, the Maker and Fashioner of the universe, through the Word who is from him, distributed, and enjoined to be in control of, the elements and the heavens and the world and what is in it, and to maintain order" (*Leg.* 10; cf. 24). We shall later see that Athenagoras has a rather clear conception of the Trinity. Here it is enough to point out that he discusses the Triad rather more carefully than Justin discussed it.

It may be added that Justin's disciple Tatian has no doctrine of the Trinity at all and makes only vague allusions to the Triad. The clearest hint he gives us lies in a mention of the Spirit as "the minister of the God who suffered" (*Or.* 13 [p. 15, 6 Schwartz]). This reference suggests that as the Word-Son proceeded from the Father (as he elsewhere says he did), so the Spirit proceeded from the Son. There is a kind of chain of being, not a Trinity—or even a Triad.

About the year 180 a bishop of Antioch named Theophilus produced several apologetic books in which he endeavored to set forth the meaning of Christianity for pagan readers. Writing from Antioch, where pagan philosophy and Jewish monotheism alike were flourishing, he insists on the supremacy of the one transcendent God and treats God's Word (*logos*) and his Wisdom as subordinate agents through which God acts. Thus he can say that "God heals and gives life through his Logos and his Wisdom" and that through them he made everything. Two biblical quotations prove his point. Psalm 32 (33 Hebrew):6 says that "by the Word (*logos*) of the Lord the heavens were made firm, and by the breath (*pneuma*) of his mouth all their power." This verse shows that for Theophilus Wisdom must really be identical with the Spirit (*pneuma*) of whom Christians ordinarily spoke. The other passage (Prov. 3:19–20) says that "by Wisdom God established the earth."[4]

Theophilus makes more of an attempt to set forth the relations between the persons when he comes to his second book. There he begins with Stoic psychology, which differentiated reason, as the *logos endiathetos*, from the spoken expression of thought, the *logos prophorikos*. Originally God had his reason within him; he generated his Word, along with his Wisdom, and created everything through him. So the Logos is properly called "beginning" in Proverbs 8:27–29 (though this passage refers to Wisdom, not to Logos) and Spirit of God and Wisdom and "power of the Most High" (as in Luke's story of the conception of Jesus, Luke 1:35).[5] Unless Theophilus is completely confused, we must assume that what he means is that before the incarnation one could speak indiscriminately about God's Word and his Wisdom; they were not clearly differentiated, since both were expressions of his mind.[6] Later on he

---

[4] *Ad Autolycum* 1, 7; according to Origen (*De princ.* 4, 4, 3 [p. 382 Koetschau]) Psalm 32:6 contains "the whole mystery of the Trinity."

[5] *Ad Autol.* 2, 10.

[6] Both Theophilus and, after him, Irenaeus regard the Word and the Wisdom of God as God's "offspring" and "hands" (Irenaeus,

quotes the first three verses of the Gospel of John and says that they show that originally God existed alone, with his *logos* within him; the word was God and was of God's nature (*ek theou pephykos*). After God expressed the Word he could send him anywhere, for unlike God himself the Word could be present in time and space.[7]

It would appear that Theophilus is so much of an apologist that he cannot (at least in his extant works) be a theologian. In the third book, when he tells us what Christians "confess," we find that they confess one God, creator and maker and fashioner of this whole universe, governing it by providence (3, 9). He says nothing of the Son or of the Holy Spirit at this point, and while we know that for him the Word was God's Son, the ambiguities in his thought about the Spirit suggest rather definitely that he has no real conception of the Trinity. He does mention a Triad of God and his Word and his Wisdom (2, 15); but when he implies that there is a Tetrad formed when man is added to the Triad, it is clear that Triad does not mean Trinity. When we notice that Theophilus mentions the Triad only because it is symbolized by the first three days in the creation story, and mentions it only in discussing the fourth day, we realize that his intense emphasis on traditional monotheism and his lack of real interest in philosophical theology have prevented him from thinking much about the Trinity. In this regard he was

---

Adv. haer. 4, 8, 1, p. 164, identifies them precisely as the Son and the Spirit). On this point see the note in A. Rousseau *et al., Irénée de Lyon: Contre les hérésies, Livre IV* (Paris, 1965), 212–19.
    [7] *Ad Autol.* 2, 22.

probably like many Christians of his time. It was enough for them to know that there is a Triad of Father, Son, and Holy Spirit. They were not concerned with interrelations; at any rate, no such concern is expressed in their extant writings.

We may wonder, then, why anyone did come to be concerned with such questions. The kind of problem involved was certainly in the air. The satirist Lucian, indeed, tells us that some persons "invoked a certain 'first god' but distributed second and third roles to other gods" (*Icaromenippus* 9). Lucian certainly has philosophers in mind, but as we shall see the problem was also considered, and of course solved, among the Gnostics.

The most important philosophical discussion was provided by a Platonist named Numenius of Apamea, who seems to have flourished during the first half of the second century. Numenius was highly regarded by such Christian writers as Clement of Alexandria and Origen. The former tells us that Numenius rhetorically asked, "What is Plato but a Moses speaking good Greek?"[8] The latter says that Numenius counted the Jews among those who taught that God is incorporeal. More precisely, Numenius provided quotations from the Old Testament prophets and interpreted them allegorically, and he recounted stories about both Jesus—without naming him—and Moses.[9] Christian theologians who encountered the thought of such a sympathetic philoso-

[8] E.-A. Leemans, *Studie over den Wijsgeer Numenius van Apamea* (Brussels, 1937), T(estimonium) 10 (Clement, *Str.* 1, 150, 4).
[9] *Ibid.*, T 9 and 19 (Origen, *Contra Celsum* 1, 15; 4, 51).

pher undoubtedly believed that he had something to say to them.

What he did say was that there is a first God who is completely unknown, and a second God, known to men, who is the Demiurge. The first sows the seed of every soul, while the second plants, distributes, and transplants.[10] The first is motionless, while the second moves; the first is related to intelligent beings, while the second is related to beings possessed both of intelligence and sense perception.[11] The first, the fashioner of being, is good-in-itself, while the fashioner of existence (*genesis*) is merely good.[12]

The fifth-century Neoplatonist Proclus tells us that in Numenius' view there are three gods: Father, Demiurge, and Cosmos. As the second God imitates the first, so the cosmos imitates the goodness of both—because it was fashioned by the first through the second.[13] Rudolf Beutler has argued that in the thought of Numenius there was really no place for three, and that this notion was the result of an inference by Proclus.[14] It would appear, however, that Numenius was providing exegesis of an obscure passage in the *Second Epistle* of Plato (312 e): "Everything is about the king of the universe and everything is because of him and he is the cause of all good things. The second about the secondary, and the third about the tertiary." This text may well be the source of the ideas described by Lucian; it would appear that it was the source of Numenius'

---

[10] *Ibid.*, F(ragmentum) 22.   [11] *Ibid.*, F 24.
[12] *Ibid.*, F 25.   [13] *Ibid.*, F 25.
[14] A. Pauly and G. Wissowa, *Realencyclopädie der classischen Altertumswissenschaft, Supplementband* VII (Stuttgart, 1940), 672.

definite mention of "the first God" and "the second and third," which occurs in a fragment preserved by Eusebius.[15]

Exegesis of the Platonic passage was widespread in the second and third centuries. Among Christians we find Justin quoting, and indeed misquoting, the words about the "second" and the "third" and referring them to the Logos and to the Spirit borne over the waters at creation (Gen. 1:3).[16] It is hard to believe that he would have encountered the passage had his attention not been drawn to it by a Platonist. Similarly Clement of Alexandria explicitly refers it to "the holy Triad,"[17] as does Eusebius, both when following Clement[18] and when composing independently.[19] On the other hand, Athenagoras quotes the whole passage but does not say what it means;[20] Origen tells us that the anti-Christian writer Celsus quoted it to show that Plato anticipated Christian doctrine, but refrains from explaining it himself.[21] Hippolytus says that the Gnostic teacher Valentinus used it as the source of his doctrine—but he is always looking for the philosophical sources of Gnosticism, not always intelligently.[22] Finally, Plotinus took it to refer to three degrees of reality: the One, beyond being; the Mind-Demiurge; and something like the cosmos.[23]

These passages show, almost conclusively, that the Christian idea that in the *Second Epistle* Plato spoke about the Triad (one might almost say Trinity except that Justin does not possess such a doctrine) was pro-

[15] F 20; Eusebius, *P.E.* 11, 18, 3.
[16] *Apol.* 1, 60, 6–7; cf. Smoroński, *op. cit.*, 275–76.
[17] *Str.* 5, 103, 1.   [18] *P.E.* 13, 13, 29.   [19] *P.E.* 11, 20, 1–3.
[20] *Leg.* 23, 8.   [21] *Contra Celsum* 6, 18.   [22] *Ref.* 6, 37, 2 and 5.
[23] *Enn.* 5, 1, 8 (quoted by Eusebius, *P.E.* 11, 17, 9).

vided by Numenius at first or second remove. On the other hand, Justin, the first Christian to quote this passage from Plato, did not develop any of the Numenian implications in the direction of a doctrine of the Trinity, and we therefore cannot say that Christian doctrine was influenced by Numenius at this point. His conception of the unity of the Demiurge with the first God was doubtless helpful to them, but they already had found such unity expressed in the Gospel of John.

If we now turn to the Gnostics we may probably discount what Hippolytus says about the origin of Valentinian doctrine. Elsewhere he ascribes it to a vision which Valentinus had.[24] Although it is true that the Gnostics often presented speculations about divine triads or even triune beings, it is hard to see how their teaching could have influenced Christians. The more mythological triads are unlike that of the Christians; the triads which come closer to Christian doctrine are almost self-evidently based upon it. A representative of the more mythological Gnosis is the *Apocryphon* (or "secret book") *of John,* of which one Coptic version is preserved at Berlin and three more have been found at Nag Hammadi in Egypt. Something like this book was known to Irenaeus, toward the end of the second century. According to it, a "unity of many forms" appeared to the apostle John and asked him why he doubted or was afraid. "I am the one who is with you always," the unity said to him. "I am the Father; I am the Mother; I am the Son."[25] Elsewhere in the book

[24] Hippolytus, *Ref.* 6, 42, 2.
[25] W. Till, *Die gnostischen Schriften des koptischen Papyrus Berolinensis 8502 (Texte und Untersuchungen* 60; Berlin, 1955), p.

these are called "the eternal three: the Father, the Mother, the Son, the perfect power."[26] And according to Irenaeus the powers above "sing hymns to the great Aeon from which were made manifest the Mother, the Father, and the Son."[27] This triad is self-evidently not Christian. It is derived from speculation about the mysteries of sex and marriage, not from meditation on the religious phenomena whose development we have tried to trace. It has nothing to do—except verbally— with the Christian Triad.

In another Gnostic group, on the other hand, there is an obvious acceptance of Christian language. "Those who are reborn," says the Valentinian Theodotus, "die to the world but live to God, so that death may be destroyed by death and perishability by resurrection. For he who has been 'sealed' [at baptism] through Father, Son, and Holy Spirit is no longer subject to the attack of any other power; by the three names he has been separated from the whole triad which lies in [the realm of] perishability."[28] This text is especially interesting because on the surface it is so straightforwardly Christian, although we wonder what the lower triad may consist of. The text implies that there is a Triad above—Father, Son, and Holy Spirit—although nothing is said of their interrelations at this point.

Theodotus, as we have noted, was a Valentinian, but

21, lines 19–21; cf. S. Giversen, *Apocryphon Johannis* (Copenhagen, 1963), plate 48, lines 6–9 (also p. 156).

[26] M. Krause and P. Labib, *Die drei Versionen des Apokryphon des Johannes im Koptischen Museum zu Alt-Kairo* (Wiesbaden, 1962), 133 (plate 57, lines 10–11).

[27] *Adv. haer.* 1, 29, 3 (p. 224 Harvey).

[28] Clement, *Excerpta ex Theodoto* 80, 2–3.

there were other Valentinians who produced a strange combination of motifs strictly Gnostic and strictly Christian. Among them we find a baptismal formula which weirdly echoes the Christian one. "Into the name of the unknown Father of all; into Truth, the Mother of all; into the one who came down to Jesus; into unity and redemption and communion with the powers."[29] This can hardly be anything but a deliberate revision, one might almost say "parody," of a Christian baptismal creed. "I believe in the Father, in the Son, in the Holy Spirit; I believe in one church, the remission of sins, and the communion of saints."[30] For Father, Son, and Holy Spirit have been substituted Father, Mother, and someone who (we know from the gospels which the Gnostics too read) is the Holy Spirit.[31]

I have mentioned the work of philosophers and Gnostics not to indicate that either group contributed anything to the religious significance of the Triad but to suggest that they reflect the kinds of frameworks, usable or not, in which speculation about the Triad as Trinity could have been set. There was one more historical factor which gave impetus to doctrinal development. This was the often repeated charge made by pagans to the effect that Christians were essentially godless or were "atheists" because they did not worship the gods of the state. In response to such charges

[29] Irenaeus, *Adv. haer.* 1, 21, 3 (pp. 183–84 Harvey).

[30] T. Barns in *Journal of Theological Studies* 6 (1904–5), 406–8. Cf. F.-M. Sagnard, *La gnose valentinienne et le témoignage de saint Irénée* (Paris, 1947), 422, n. 2.

[31] We may add that the Peratae, who held that there were three gods, also stated that "the whole" consists of Father, Son, and matter (Hippolytus, *Ref.* 5, 17, 2).

Christians had to state their own doctrine of God as clearly as possible.

Thus we find Athenagoras explicitly replying to the charge when he states who the God of the Christians is (*Leg.* 10). They worship

[1] the one uncreated, eternal, invisible, impassible, incomprehensible, uncontainable God; comprehensible only by mind and reason;[32] surrounded by inexpressible light and beauty and spirit and power; by whom the universe was made through his Word [or, Reason] and was given form and is held together [cf. Col. 1:17, 2:19, Eph. 4:16];

[2] the Son of God, who is the Word [or, Reason] of the Father in idea and activity; in relation to him (πρὸς αὐτοῦ) and through him everything came into existence [John 1:1–3], since the Father and the Son are one [John 10:30; 17:11]; since the Son is in the Father and the Father is in the Son [John 10:38; 14:10–11; 14:20; 17:21], in the unity and power of the Spirit [cf. John 16:13–15; I John 3:24], the Son of God is the Mind and Word [or, Reason] of the Father [Athenagoras also explains that the Mind of God always contains Reason, but that Reason came forth from him for created beings; he confirms this point by a quotation from Proverbs 8:22]; and

[3] the Holy Spirit, emanated from God, emanating and borne along like a ray of the sun [Wisdom 7:25–26].

How can anyone call Christians atheists, Athenagoras asks, when they speak of God the Father and God the Son and the Holy Spirit? Christians point to the power of the persons in their unity and their distinctiveness in rank. Here, with whatever imprecision of language is present, we finally encounter a carefully worked-out doctrine of the Trinity.

It is of the highest importance that although some of

---

[32] The same idea is ascribed to Plato by Justin (*Dial.* 3, 7); cf. Albinus, *Didasc.* 10 (p. 165 Hermann).

the language used by Athenagoras sounds philosophical, and some of it *is* philosophical, the basic structure of his thought is latently biblical and is derived especially from the New Testament. The idea that the world is held together by God through the pre-existent Christ comes from Colossians and Ephesians. The expressions used of the creation through the Word and of the unity of the Father with the Son are certainly based on the Gospel of John. And the language Athenagoras uses of the Spirit comes from the Book of Wisdom, in his time and later highly valued among Alexandrian Christians.

There is a certain ambiguity, later to produce difficulties especially during the Arian crisis, about the use of passages which in the Old Testament refer to the Wisdom of God. Thus Athenagoras refers the Wisdom of Proverbs 8:22 to the Son and the Wisdom of the Book of Wisdom to the Spirit. Such a bifurcation reflects a weakness in exegesis which has resulted in a weakness in theology. More precisely, it reflects an unclear analysis of the nature and functions of the Holy Spirit—but we cannot expect a second-century apologist to solve the problems which produced violent controversies several centuries later.

In my opinion, the judgment of both Harnack and Geffcken—the one a great historian of dogma, the other a great student of early Christianity from the standpoint of classical philology—deserves assent. Geffcken quotes Harnack on the importance of Athenagoras' presentation. As to the nature of its importance I venture to disagree. Harnack said that Athenagoras was the only apologist "to eliminate the existence of the Logos in time and to emphasize the eternal character of the divine relationships."[33] This is one way of looking at it, and one must admit that like other apologists Athenagoras has little or nothing to say about the life of Jesus, though he does regard him as a teacher and quotes some of his teachings. Unless one looks very carefully at the text of Theophilus and reads between the lines, one finds almost nothing about Jesus. Neither he nor Tatian nor Minucius Felix nor Athenagoras himself ever mentions the name Jesus or Christ, and oddly enough it is also absent from the *Shepherd* of Hermas (in James it occurs only twice). There is something of an apologetic convention here. In an apologetic writing you do not usually argue on your own grounds, at least explicitly; you try to choose ground common to yourself and your opponent and see if you can gradually move him in your direction. This, I believe, is what has happened in Athenagoras' writing.

Now it is at this point that the historian of Christian doctrine encounters grave difficulties which he often passes over lightly. Do the early Christian documents we possess, especially if they are second-century apologies, really and fully reflect the Christian faith of those who wrote them? I believe that one must answer this question in several ways. First, the writers are not likely to make any statements they themselves view as false or incorrect. The statements may be incomplete and partial, but they will not be intentionally misleading. In addition, the philosophical language by means of which the writers interpret Christianity is a language to which they are personally committed. As we indicated

[33] J. Geffcken, *Zwei griechische Apologeten* (Leipzig-Berlin, 1907), 181, quoting A. Harnack, *Dogmengeschichte*, I, 488ff.

in the first essay in this volume there is a long tradition of philosophical terminology within Christianity, and there was no reason for the writers to abandon it. They evidently believed that it was possible for them to use the current philosophical language in setting forth certain aspects, at least, of their gospel. Second, as we have already indicated, most of them used a certain measure of reserve. Their goal was in effect educational. They did not believe in starting the course at the end. Third, in order to understand their thought more fully we must read between the lines and must remember that not every Christian writer felt it necessary to produce a complete systematic theology, or even a complete account of the Christian religion. We must remember that all of them wrote out of the context of a community, in which God was not simply discussed but also was worshiped; in which the story of his dealings with men was constantly reread. Christians read parts of the Old Testament and what was coming to be the New Testament; they took part in liturgical prayer and nonliturgical prayer; they tried actually to live lives they regarded as Christian.

One might suppose that these points would be obvious were it not that they are so often neglected. There were theological change and development, but they took place against a fairly constant background of baptism and eucharist, prayer and thanksgiving, preaching and action. This point can be proved from the strictly apologetic fragments of Melito of Sardis, combined with the vividly rhetorical but firmly religious paschal sermon first discovered only in 1940.[34] From the

[34] C. Bonner, *The Homily on the Passion by Melito Bishop of*

apologetic fragments one could never have guessed how Melito spoke when he preached within the community.

At the same time, one must also beware of reading back too much into the earlier documents. Change and development actually were characteristic of the Christian churches and their leaders, and unless this movement had existed one could not imagine how or why the conflicts among groups were as conspicuous and constant as they actually were. We must not imagine that there was a golden age, or that a doctrine of the Trinity such as we have found in Athenagoras' writings had always existed in the Christian subconscious.

The doctrine of the Trinity, for Athenagoras and for later Christians, represented an attempt to do justice to the unity of God and the diversity of God's dealings with men. The unity of God was based squarely on the testimony of the Old Testament and of the New Testament as well. Jesus, no less than the prophets, had proclaimed the unity and the sole rule of God, and the apostles shared in his proclamation. In and after his resurrection the apostles and their successors came to be convinced that his mission had been and would be an eternal mission. Since he had been exalted to God's right hand, he had come thence originally. Since he was God's agent in redemption, the new creation, in God's purpose he must always have been the agent of God. But what other agent could God need or have than

---

Sardis (London, 1940); B. Lohse, *Die Passa-Homilie des Bischofs Meliton von Sardes* (Leiden, 1958); M. Testuz, *Papyrus Bodmer XIII: Méliton de Sardes, Homélie sur la Pâque* (Coligny-Geneva, 1960).

himself? It was the attempt to answer a question like this that led to the Christological doctrines of the Fourth Gospel and the second century.

The early Christians were also aware of the presence of a new power among themselves, a power which they called the Holy Spirit and identified with the Spirit which spoke through the prophets; some of them had predicted that in the last days this Spirit would be poured out upon men. They could call the Spirit the Spirit of God or the Spirit of Christ, but they gradually came to differentiate its workings from those of Christ (though they never separated them entirely) as they laid more emphasis on Christ's work as effected during the time of his incarnation. To some extent this emphasis reflects the recognition that the world was not going to come to an end; it reflects a movement which can be called a transition from apocalyptic thought to philosophy or to Catholicity.

The development of the doctrine of the Trinity took place in the world of Graeco-Roman philosophy, but as I have tried to show the philosophy did not produce the doctrine. The philosophical thought was used as a means to work out some of the implications of the religious realities (Father, Son, and Holy Spirit) which Christians already knew.

In modern times there have been many critics of the traditional formulations of the doctrine. Some have felt that to call Jesus the Son of God is not satisfactory; others have attacked the differentiation between Jesus and the Spirit; a few have felt that a better modern archetype would be provided by a family consisting of Father, Mother, and Child. Some opponents have gone so far as to suggest that what modern man needs is just the figure of Jesus, apart from the irrelevant Father whom he happened to proclaim. From what I have said it should be fairly clear that I do not agree with any of these propositions. At the same time, it is fairly evident that the precise modes of thought employed by the early Christian writers have no claim to eternity or perpetuation. All of them—and among "all" I should include the New Testament writers as well—were conditioned by the modes of thought which to them seemed self-evident, whether they were Jewish or Greek or Roman. This is to say that the precise formulations provided by the early Christian writers have little claim upon us. It is their "detached insights," as Whitehead once said of ancient thinkers generally, that are "priceless." But if one is going to speak of "detached insights" in relation to these writers, one must ask, "Detached insights of what?"

Here we arrive at what I must claim is the final and necessary step to be taken by the historian of doctrine. He must finally pass beyond the role of observer and reporter, important and indispensable though this is; he must ask what reality he can believe lies behind the external phenomena with which he has dealt. To put it another way, why study the early development of the doctrine of the Trinity if it provides an example of what a college president once defined to me as "the rubbish the churches have added"? The answer I should give is the one I tried to present in regard to the life that lies behind and beyond the writings of the apologists. There are crucial religious realities, expressed not only in words but in events and in symbolic re-enactments of the events, which lie behind the trinitarian terminology. There is (I should agree) concretely the figure of Jesus, who not only taught men to love one another but enacted this love and fidelity in his suffering and death. There is the God to whom he pointed, the one whom he believed he was obeying, the one proclaimed through the prophets also as a God of justice, mercy, power, and love.[35] The insights expressed through the words "God" and "Christ" are intuitional insights concerning the nature of the universe and the nature of human existence. Similarly there is the Holy Spirit, which I find difficult to differentiate from the risen and exalted Lord. Perhaps one needs to speak of the Holy Spirit simply because the Lord is regarded as exalted—and here we have to beware of taking our metaphors too concretely.

At the same time, we should beware of speaking of the Trinity or, for that matter, of God as if we somehow have direct access to God or as if he is ours in the sense that we must defend him as somehow being our property. The later arguments concerning the Trinity were often conducted in such a way as to suggest that ecclesiastical politics could be a substitute for Christian charity. The word "heresy" should not be bandied about by those whose Christian community was once a sect within Judaism; the word "atheism" should not be used lightly by the modern successors of those who in the Roman empire were viewed as atheists.

[35] Cf. Origen, *Contra Celsum* 7, 43: "God the Father is seen not only in accordance with 'Blessed are the pure in heart, for they shall see God' [Matt. 5:8], but also in accordance with what was said by the image of the invisible God [Col. 1:15]: 'He who has seen me has seen the Father' [John 14:9]."

It seems to me that the doctrine of the Trinity can be viewed as the product of an attempt to find unity behind the multiplicity of human experience—a unity which would not be a "bare" or reductionist unity but one which would transcend the multiplicity while not denying its reality. Perhaps if Christians were to pay more attention to the richness and diversity of trinitarian thought, the notion that "God is dead" would be less exciting. In a certain sense, indeed, though with many qualifying statements along the way, the Christian who believes in the Trinity can also say, not that God is dead, but that God has died; in other words, God himself has entered, in his Son, into the boundary zone of human experience—though the Christian would have to add with Paul that "Christ being raised from the dead dieth no more; death hath no more dominion over him" (Rom. 5:9). More than most others, Christians have insisted upon the reality of death, though they have gone on to speak of triumph over it.

And yet, though I dislike the vulgar use of the word "heresy," it would appear that less than justice is done to the crucial Christian concerns when anyone lays all his emphasis on one person of the Trinity at the expense of the others. Throughout the history of Christian thought there have been men who venerated only one of the persons, as H. Richard Niebuhr once pointed out in an incisive article.[36] There have been "practical monotheisms" not only of the Father but also of the Son and of the Holy Spirit. As witnesses to rather extreme emphasis on the Son at the expense of the other persons,

[36] "The Doctrine of the Trinity and the Unity of the Church," *Theology Today* 3 (1946–47), 371–84.

he mentioned the theologies of Marcion, of Sweden-
borg, and even of Ritschl and Herrmann, as well as such
a hymn as "Fairest Lord Jesus."[37] As witnesses to
exaggerated devotion to the Spirit, he referred to Joachim de Fiore, Roger Williams, adherents of an inner
light, and representatives of nineteenth-century ideal-
ism. It is not that devotion to any one of the persons is
wrong. It is simply that it is partial and, indeed, inadequate. For God is not only Redeemer but also Creator
and Judge; he is not only inspirer to moral action and to
mystical communion but also Lord of nature and history and one who became involved in both nature and
history. The three persons correspond to the experience
and thought of Christians not only in the apostolic age
but also after it, and these Christians recognized that the
three are somehow one.

"Somehow" may seem a rather vague word. But if we
recall the emphatic insistence of second-century Christians upon the transcendence of God and the limitations
of our knowledge about him, it may well be a good
word with which to end. To speak over-precisely about
the ineffable God, to define too carefully the relations
between the Father and the Son, to produce exact
analyses of the place and function of the Spirit in the
Trinity—this is to set ourselves up as judges of God and

[37] He might also have referred to the second-century Carpocra-
tians, who had images of Jesus which, they claimed, were copies of
one made by Pilate; they put crowns on them and placed them
with images of Pythagoras, Plato, and Aristotle (Irenaeus, *Adv.
haer.* 1, 25, 5 [p. 210 Harvey]). Similarly the third-century
emperor Alexander Severus venerated statues of the best of the
deified emperors along with those of Apollonius of Tyana, Christ,
Abraham, and Orpheus (*Scriptores historiae Augustae, Severus
Alexander* 29, 2).

to forget that his ways are not like ours. It may still be significant that early Christians most often mentioned the Triad in connection with their worship, in baptism, eucharist, and in doxologies addressed to the Father through the Son and in the Holy Spirit.

It would be improper to end these essays with a word about Christian worship, even though it is in acts of worship that the Triad and the Trinity are most often named, for the "essence of Christianity"—even for the early Christians—seems to lie in its affirmation that God is not the God of Christians alone. He is the God of the universe, who so loved the world that he sent his Son to redeem it; the Holy Spirit is not confined within the church but has cosmic functions. "The Christian God" is a bad expression not only in relation to the history of philosophical theology but also in relation to Christianity—and to other religions.[38] The doctrine of the Trinity represents an attempt to understand the mystery of the Triad, but its earlier formulations may be too closely related not only to Graeco-Roman philosophy but also to Christian experience alone. We are not called to turn our backs upon the life of the Christian community either past or present. In future interpretations of the work of God, however, we are bound to take into account the all-inclusive love of the transcendent One, dimly perceived by us as Father, Son, and Holy Spirit, but ultimately making himself known to all men in religious languages which they can understand.

[38] On this problem in philosophical theology cf. J. W. Keating in *Harvard Theological Review* 58 (1965), 417–26.

Appendixes

10

PROOFS OF THE UNITY OF GOD

ONE of the most interesting passages in the *Legatio* of Athenagoras occurs in the eighth chapter, where the apologist states that he is providing a rational proof (*logismos*) of the Christian faith. By this he means that he is demonstrating the absolute oneness of God. Modern responses to his demonstration have not always been very favorable. Geffcken called it "a clumsy improvisation on the theme," and Puech said that "in spite of its apparent rigor the manner of argument is rather weak." Richardson is more generous, and Crehan contents himself with describing it as *reductio ad absurda*.[1] Here

[1] J. Geffcken, *Zwei griechische Apologeten* (Leipzig-Berlin, 1907), 179; A. Puech, *Les apologistes grecs* (Paris, 1912), 185; C. C.

we are concerned with three interrelated questions: (1) What models did Athenagoras possess? (2) How did he modify them? (3) Why did he modify them?

At the outset we must reject the statement of A. Bill to the effect that ancient philosophy was not sharply enough opposed to popular belief to provide proof that there was one God.[2] We do so on the ground of four examples. (1) Philo of Alexandria (*Conf. ling.* 170) argues that since no existent thing is in origin equal to God, and since the *Iliad* (2, 204–5) rejects the idea of a multiplicity of rulers and is referring to the cosmos and to God, therefore there must be one Maker, Father, and Master of the one cosmos. It seems strange for Philo to be proving his point from the *Iliad*, and we therefore infer that at this juncture he is incorporating a bit of Hellenistic philosophical exegesis of Homer into his text. (2) Specifically, this doctrine is Stoic. Plutarch (*De def. orac.* 23–30, 422c–426e) criticizes the Stoics for holding that as there are one destiny and one providence (and one cosmos), so there are not several gods or Zeuses to govern several worlds.[3] Ultimately their doctrine goes back to Aristotle's argument that since there is one order of nature there must be one creator (*Metaphys.* 10).[4] (3) In the eleventh treatise of

Richardson, *Early Christian Fathers* (Philadelphia, 1953), 295; J. Crehan, *Athenagoras* (Westminster, Md., 1956), 131.

[2] A. Bill, *Zur Erklärung und Textkritik des 1. Buches Tertullians "Adversus Marcionen"* (*Texte und Untersuchungen* 38; Leipzig, 1911), 18–19.

[3] H. von Arnim, *Stoicorum veterum fragmenta* (Leipzig, 1905–24), II, 632.

[4] Cf. H. A. Wolfson, *Philo*, II (Cambridge, Mass., 1947), 98–100.

the *Corpus Hermeticum* it is argued that the existence of one order, with all the multiplicity in it, requires the postulation of one creator; that there would be jealousy if there were two or more creators; that the work of governing the creative activity could not be shared by two; and that as the soul is one so God is one.[5] (4) In the Graeco-Roman treatise ascribed to Aristotle and entitled *De Melisso Xenophane Gorgia* we find an elaborate argument attributed to Xenophanes.[6] First, God cannot come into being. Things that come into being do so from origins either similar or dissimilar; but God has no origin either similar or dissimilar; therefore he is eternal. Second, "if there were two or more, he [God] would no longer be most powerful and best of all." If there were more than one, and they were unequal, they would not be gods because the nature of the divine is such as not to be overpowered. If they were equal, they would not have the nature of God. Therefore if God exists he is one alone.

The last of these arguments seems to lie at the base of Athenagoras' demonstration. To be sure, the pseudo-Xenophanes goes on to argue that God is spherical and Athenagoras does not follow him at this point; but it may be significant that the Christian apologist does claim (perhaps under the influence of this source) that

[5] See the summary in A. D. Nock and A.-J. Festugière, *Corpus Hermeticum*, I (Paris, 1945), 144–45.

[6] H. Diels, *Aristotelis qui fertur de Melisso Xenophane Gorgia libellus* (*Philosophische und historische Abhandlungen der königlichen Akademie der Wissenschaften zu Berlin, 1899–1900;* Berlin, 1900, no. 1); cf. W. Jaeger, *The Theology of the Early Greek Philosophers* (Oxford, 1947), 51–55.

if the world is spherical and is encompassed by the spheres of heaven there is no place for gods other than the one.

Athenagoras' argument runs as follows: If there were two or more gods they would belong either to the same genus or to different genera. (I) If they belonged to the same genus, they would be either equal or unequal. (A) If they were equal, they would be similar to each other and, if they came into existence, would be based on a prior model. But as gods they did not come into existence; there was no model prior to them; they are dissimilar and unequal and do not belong to the same genus. (B) It might be held that they are dissimilar and unequal but to be regarded as gods because, like parts of the human body, they are complementary. This view is untenable because only what comes into existence and perishes is divisible into parts, whereas by definition God does not come into existence and is impassible and indivisible. Therefore they cannot be complementary— or dissimilar and unequal. Athenagoras concludes that two or more gods could not belong to the same genus. (II) If, on the other hand, they belong to different genera, there cannot be two or more of them because there would be no function or location for a god or gods other than the God who created this universe and governs it. If another god were to rule another universe, he would not be God, for his power would be limited by the power the Creator exercises here; he would not be omnipotent. Therefore, Athenagoras concludes, there is one God the Creator.

It is evident that this argument contains a good many assumptions, which in Athenagoras' opinion are both

Platonic and Christian. He tells us that the Christian doctrine is that "the divine is uncreated and eternal, visible only to mind and reason, while matter is created and perishable" (*Leg.* 4), and that Plato taught that there is one Demiurge, the uncreated God (*Leg.* 6). In Athenagoras' view the true God obviously exercises providential care and is omnipotent. Indeed, the whole argument could have been based on omnipotence, for obviously only one God could be omnipotent.

The basic question which arises concerning his argument is why he speaks of God's location in Part II. Puech noted that "in speaking of the place in which the Deity resides, the author proves how difficult it is to deal with the concept of an immaterial being, even though it is easy to raise it in principle."[7] We therefore ask why Athenagoras does so—though it could be Stoic in origin as we have seen in the first parallel cited above.

A clue is probably given us when we find Irenaeus using a somewhat similar argument against the Valentinians and, more important, both Tertullian and the author of the *Dialogue of Adamantius* employing a strikingly similar one against the Marcionites.[8] In Marcion's opinion there were two first principles, both of them self-produced and limitless, both of them gods.[9] Like Athenagoras, Tertullian argues that the *summum magnum* must be *unicum*. Unlike man, God is indivisible. Again, Marcion held that the Demiurge was an

---

[7] Puech, *op. cit.*, 185.

[8] Irenaeus, *Adv. haer.* 2, 1, 1 (p. 251 Harvey); Tertullian, *Adversus Marcionem* 1, 3–11; *Dial. Adamant.* 2, 1–2.

[9] *Dial. Adamant.* 2, 1; Tertullian, *Adv. Marc.* 3, 15.

infinite distance below the true God, and that only the Demiurge ruled the cosmos here below.[10] Yet, as Tertullian pointed out, the Demiurge exercised no providential care; he was actually *otiosus* (*Adv. Marc.* 5, 4).

Athenagoras' argument, with its lengthy discussion of places and functions, seems to find a *Sitz im Leben* if at least in part, and perhaps as a whole, it was originally produced as a semiphilosophical reply to Marcion and then was used again in relation to philosophy. We know that in his time the problems raised by Marcion concerned many Christian writers, and that in the apologetic treatises of his contemporary Theophilus of Antioch anti-Marcionite arguments appear along the way.

Relying primarily on philosophical antecedents, then, Athenagoras created an argument first for use against Marcionites, later for a defense of monotheism in an environment he viewed as close to philosophy.

[10] Irenaeus, *Adv. haer.* 4, 33, 2; 1, 27, 2.

THE IMPASSIBILITY
OF GOD

ONE of the words we have frequently encountered in reference to God is *apathēs*, "impassible." It does not occur in the New Testament, though Ignatius of Antioch uses it in speaking of the divine nature of Christ (*Eph.* 7, 2; *Polyc.* 3, 2). Justin employs it not only of God (*Apol.* 25, 2) and in a definition ("the incorporeal is impassible," *Dial.* 1, 5) but also in regard to Christians. If they keep the commandments, they become like God, impassible and immortal (*Dial.* 124, 4); like Christ, they live in impassibility (2 *Apol.* 1, 2).[1] Similarly, Athenagoras speaks both of God (*Leg.* 8, 2; 10,

---

[1] Cf. also *Apol.* 10, 2; 57, 2; 58, 3; *Dial.* 46, 7.

1) and of Christians' lives with him (*Leg.* 31, 3) as characterized by impassibility.

Irenaeus held that God is impassible (*Adv. haer.* 2, 17, 6) and maintained that the Logos too, derived from him, is perfect and impassible (2, 17, 7). Against the Docetists, however, he firmly maintained that Christ truly suffered (3, 18, 6).[2] He could not accept the Gnostic view that the Saviour-Spirit of Christ remained impassible and could not suffer because it was undominated and invisible (1, 7, 2) or that while Jesus suffered and was raised, the Christ remained impassible, since he was spiritual (1, 26, 1).

In the writings of Clement of Alexandria impassibility is characteristic both of God and of the image of God (*Str.* 5, 54, 5). The Son was impassible; "he could never abandon his care for mankind through the distractions of any pleasure, since after he had taken on the flesh, which is by nature subject to passion, he trained it to habitual impassibility" (7, 7, 5). In some of his remarks on this subject Clement comes very close to Docetism (6, 71, 3; cf. his quotation from Valentinus in 3, 59, 3). The Christian Gnostic, too, is impassible (7, 67, 8; 7, 88, 2; *Quis dives salvetur* 20, 6). Clement shrinks back, however, from identifying divine and human impassibility. The Christian Gnostic may be called perfect, but he is by no means similar to God. "For we do not agree with the impious opinion of the Stoics as to the identity of divine and human virtue.[3]

[2] On the Christological problem cf. A. Houssiau, *La christologie de saint Irénée* (Louvain, 1955), 190.

[3] Von Arnim, *Stoicorum veterum fragmenta*, III, 245–54 (Clement's statement provides Fragment 250).

Perhaps then we ought to be as perfect as the Father wishes us to be; for it is impossible and impracticable that anyone should be as perfect as God."[4] One may say, therefore, that Clement's insistence upon divine *apatheia* is in part due to the absolute differentiation he makes between God and man.

Origen held the opposite opinion about human virtue. "The virtue of man and God is the same. That is why we are taught to become 'perfect as our heavenly Father is perfect' (Matt. 5:48)." The anti-Christian writer Celsus had said that Christians and Jews were like worms, ants, frogs, and bats, croaking in concert (do worms and ants croak?) as to which of them were the worst sinners. Origen replied that noble, good, righteous, and illuminated men were in no way similar to these species of animals.[5] He clearly held the Stoic view that divine and human virtue are one.[6]

To be sure, even in his late *Commentary on Matthew* Origen referred to *apatheia* as practically the crown of the virtues[7] and said that Christians must remain impassible until the coming of Christ in glory;[8] but from his *Homily on Ezekiel* we have already seen (page 30) that his doctrine was not absolutely rigid.

The rigorist position was certainly held by Philo, who strongly influenced the Alexandrian theologians; he stated that Moses advocated not moderation but absolute *apatheia*.[9] This was the Stoic view, at least

---

[4] *Str.* 7, 88, 5–6; cf. *Str.* 2, 135, 3; 6, 114, 5.
[5] *Contra Celsum* 4, 29.
[6] *Ibid.*, 6, 48.
[7] *Matt. comm.* 15, 17 (p. 398, 27 Klostermann).
[8] *Matt. ser. comm.* 54 (p. 122, 27 Klostermann).
[9] *Leg. alleg.* 3, 129.

among orthodox Stoics.[10] Plotinus too often spoke of divine and human *apatheia*.[11] This philosophical atmosphere undoubtedly did early Christian theology no good.

[10] The orthodox view: von Arnim, *op. cit.*, III, 443–55 (especially Fragment 448, Diogenes Laertius 7, 117). Modification: e.g., Seneca, *Ep.* 1, 9, 3; Epictetus, *Diss.* 3, 2, 4.

[11] According to Eusebius, *H.E.* 6, 8, 1–3, Origen castrated himself; Porphyry (*Vita Plotini* 1) said that Plotinus was ashamed of being in a body.

III

THE DEVELOPMENT OF CHRISTOLOGY AS VIEWED IN THE EARLY CHURCH

FEW problems are of more concern to a living movement than that of defining its continuity with its origins. On the one hand, there is the obvious existence of change; on the other, there is a sameness within the change, and with the passage of time it becomes necessary to assess the relationship between the two. There is also the factor of diversity-within-unity, often found at the very beginning but more clearly evident as the movement goes on.

Even within the New Testament we find considerable diversity. One need only recall that most of the letters of the apostle Paul are explicitly directed against those whom he regards as presenting an incorrect version of Christianity. He has difficulties with his apostolic predecessors, and in 1 Corinthians 15:10 he insists that he has labored more diligently than all of them. The first two chapters of Galatians are intended to show that he was quite independent of the leaders of the church at Jerusalem and that when Cephas, a "pillar" of that church, came to Antioch he vigorously opposed him. His own revelation of Christ gave him a more adequate understanding of the gospel than that possessed by his predecessors. "Even if we have known Christ in human fashion, we no longer know him so" (2 Cor. 5:16).

In addition, the authors of the synoptic gospels frequently speak of the disciples' lack of comprehension of what Jesus said to them, and Luke makes explicit the claim that they wrongly supposed that the kingdom of God would immediately appear (19:11; cf. 24:21; Acts 1:6).[1] John sets forth the difference between the disciples' original ignorance and his own understanding by indicating that the latter arose after the resurrection (2:22; 12:16) and was due to the gift of the Holy Spirit (14:26; 15:26; 16:12-15). Both Luke and John state that after the resurrection the disciples came to understand the meaning of Old Testament prophecy (Luke 24:45; John 2:22; 12:16; 20:9).

The passage of time is quite clearly indicated in 2 Peter 3:4, where it is reported that people are questioning the reliability of apocalyptic prophecy on the ground that nature has remained constant since the beginning of creation, and in 2 Peter 3:8, where the

---

[1] Cf. H. Conzelmann, *The Theology of St. Luke* (New York, 1960).

author claims that "with the Lord one day is like a thousand years and a thousand years are like a day." A similar point had been made even earlier, for in Mark 13:32 we read that "no one, not even the angels in heaven or the Son, knows about that day or that hour; only the Father knows."

Under these conditions it was relatively easy for various Gnostic teachers of the early second century to claim that their knowledge of the authentic, secret teaching of Jesus had come to them from his favorite disciples and was not recorded, except imperfectly, in the books commonly used among Christians. Basilides, for example, claimed that his information had come from Peter's interpreter Glaukias; Valentinus said that his source was Paul's companion Theodas. The best example of "historical" analysis is provided by the Gnostic teacher Marcion. He claimed that although after the resurrection the disciples did understand Jesus they rapidly perverted the original gospel because they were trying to set it forth in terms comprehensible to Jewish hearers. A new revelation was needed to restore the original one, and this was given to the apostle Paul. Unfortunately his letters were interpolated by Judaizers, and so was the full gospel he proclaimed. By removing interpolations from his letters and by correcting the Gospel of Luke, it was possible—so Marcion believed—to get back to the authentic form of the Christian message. This kind of theory, not uncommon outside Christianity in the second century, proved to be very troublesome for defenders of continuity.[2]

On the more orthodox side we find the Book of Acts,

[2] Cf. *The Letter and the Spirit* (London, 1957), 19–23; 64.

with its insistence on the continuity between the Jerusalem church and Paul and between Paul and those whom he appointed to be in charge of various churches. The same emphasis is expressed in the letter of Clement of Rome to the Corinthians. He points out that the Corinthian church originally enjoyed complete harmony and peace (hardly the impression we should gain from Paul's letters!), although discord later set in. A little later we encounter the fragments of Papias of Hierapolis, who eagerly collected oral traditions which "were given by the Lord to the faith and came from the Truth itself" (Eusebius, *H.E.* 3, 39, 3). Obviously Papias laid great emphasis on continuity.

It was in the period between about 160 and about 180 that the question of continuity came most to the fore, since this was also the period in which the Gnostic heresy seems to have been most prevalent. Dionysius of Corinth, for example, reminds the Roman Christians that "from the beginning" their custom has been to help others (Eusebius, *H.E.* 4, 23, 10); doubtless he has in mind not only 1 Clement, which he knew, but also Paul's epistle to the Romans and perhaps 1 Peter. He knows something about the troubled history of the church at Athens. The Athenians had "all but apostatized" after the martyrdom of their bishop Publius, but his successor Quadratus (perhaps in the reign of Hadrian) had brought them together again (4, 23, 10). Dionysius also knows how difficult it is to rely on written documents. His own letters have been interpolated by "apostles of the devil," and it is therefore not remarkable if some have tampered with the "dominical scriptures" as well (4, 23, 12).

It was in about the same time that the *aedicula* in the Vatican was erected either to contain the bones of Peter or to mark the spot of his martyrdom,[3] and probably in the same decade the relics of Polycarp, bishop of Smyrna, who was viewed as a link with the apostles, were treasured by his congregation.[4]

Some time after the year 175 we begin to find historical schematization carried further. Melito of Sardis addressed an apology to the emperor and argued that because Christianity arose along with the Roman empire, in the reign of Augustus, it deserved encouragement by the state. Among the emperors only Nero and Domitian, misled by bad advisers, persecuted Christians; the ancestors of Marcus Aurelius had favored them. In proof of this favor Melito mentioned a letter sent by Antoninus Pius to Macedonians and Greeks.[5] Another Christian apologist, Hegesippus, seems to have been responsible for a periodized scheme of church history. At Corinth the church "continued in the true faith until Primus was bishop"[6]—unfortunately the date of Primus is unknown. At Jerusalem, James the Just was the first bishop, and in his time the church there was still a "virgin," i.e., not corrupted by heresy. After the death of James, Symeon (son of Clopas and nephew of Joseph) was appointed bishop, but a certain Thebuthis,

[3] Cf. J. Toynbee and J. W. Perkins, *The Shrine of St. Peter* (New York, 1957); T. Klauser, *Die römische Petrustradition im Lichte der neuen Ausgrabungen* (Cologne, 1956); H. Chadwick in *Journal of Theological Studies* 8 (1957), 31–52.

[4] The passage in *Mart. Polyc.* 18, 1–2 on relics may be late; cf. H. von Campenhausen in *Sitzungsberichte der Heidelberger Akademie der Wissenschaften*, 1957, *Philos.-hist. Kl. no.* 3, 28–31 —though in his text (p. 47) he retains it.

[5] Eusebius, *H.E.* 4, 26, 7–10.   [6] *Ibid.*, 4, 22, 1.

eager for episcopal office, began to corrupt the church with doctrines derived from sectarian Judaism. In the reign of Trajan, when Symeon was 120 years old, the heretics informed against him and he was crucified by Roman authorities. According to Hegesippus, up to this time "every church" (in Palestine) was ruled by members of the Lord's family; afterward came the rise of heresy and the development of other forms of government.[7] There was thus a golden age (the apostolic), as well as a silver one (the subapostolic); afterward heresy began to be prevalent. In essence this resembles the idea of Justin that heresy arose only after the ascension,[8] but it is more elaborately developed. Hegesippus seems to have made a list of the bishops of Rome, for apparently the Roman church was free from doctrinal disturbances.[9] (From other Christian writings, however, we know that it was not exempt from them.)

The clear periodization of Hegesippus was employed by other Christian writers. Irenaeus, for example, tells us that Polycarp, appointed bishop by apostles, was militantly opposed to Marcion, Cerinthus, and the Valentinians, all of whom were later than the apostles themselves.[10] Clement of Alexandria argues that what he calls "human conventicles" came into existence later than the Catholic church. The teaching of the Lord was given during the reigns of Augustus and Tiberius; that of the apostles lasted until, for example, the death of Paul in the reign of Nero. (Perhaps he says "for example" because he recalls that according to tradition

[7] *Ibid.*, 4, 22, 4–5; 3, 32, 6.   [8] *Apol.* 26.
[9] Eusebius, *H.E.* 4, 22, 2–3.
[10] Irenaeus, *Adv. haer.* 3, 3, 4 (p. 13 Harvey).

John did not die until the reign of Domitian, or even that of Nerva.) The founders of heresies, on the other hand, did not begin their work until the reign of Hadrian and, in some instances, continued on into the reign of Antoninus Pius. Such was the case in regard to Basilides and Valentinus (both of whom claimed apostolic sanction for their doctrines) and even the somewhat older Marcion.[11]

If we try to imagine a synthesis of the periodizations provided by Melito and Clement, we find something like the following scheme, useful against the church's enemies both internal and external. (1) There was no unorthodoxy during the lifetime of the Lord himself, during the reigns of Augustus and Tiberius; church and state lived in harmony during this period. (Our authors do not mention the actions of Pontius Pilate at this point.) (2) There was no unorthodoxy as long as the apostles continued to teach, James at Jerusalem, Peter and Paul at Rome, perhaps the long-lived John at Ephesus. Nero's persecution of Christians was due to bad advice. Insofar as heresy arose at Jerusalem after the death of James, it was due to (a) human ambition and (b) infiltrations from Jewish sects. (3) Probably orthodoxy was preserved in most places as long as the apostles' immediate successors, or the successors of these men, remained in office. Then, in the reign of Hadrian, a wave of heresy swept over the church, although Rome remained a bulwark of orthodoxy. At Jerusalem heretics caused the persecution of the church by the state. Probably we should place the episcopates of Publius of Athens and Primus of Corinth in this period.

[11] Clement, *Str.* 7, 106, 3–107, 1.

Given the existence of a scheme like this, there was precedent for doctrinal discussions at Rome in the early third century, when heresy vigorously flourished, especially in regard to the doctrine of Christ as God and man. Zephyrinus, bishop of Rome, contributed to the confusion. Sometimes, according to his opponent Hippolytus, he would say, "I know one God Jesus Christ and apart from him no other, created and passible." On other occasions he would state that "it was not the Father who died, but the Son."[12] Against him and others the followers of Artemon maintained that Jesus was a man who had been adopted by God as his Son, and they provided a sketch of the history of doctrine: "All the men of former days, and the apostles themselves, received and taught the things which we now say. The truth of the preaching was preserved until the times of Victor, who was the thirteenth bishop at Rome from Peter, but the truth was falsified from the days of his successor Zephyrinus." In reply, an orthodox writer (possibly Hippolytus) proceeded to list doctrinal authorities to show that his own view was traditional. Three second-century apologists (Justin, Miltiades, and Tatian) and Clement of Alexandria had spoken of Christ as God, while both Irenaeus and Melito had said that he was both God and man. These doctrines were also to be found both in the scriptures and in the "psalms or songs" of the church.[13]

In other words, the orthodox writer maintains the continuity of Christian doctrine while the unorthodox

[12] Hippolytus, *Ref.* 9, 11, 3.
[13] Eusebius, *H.E.* 5, 28, 3–4. In addition, the antiheretical writer claimed that Victor of Rome had excommunicated an adherent of the Artemonite view.

writer also maintains it but claims that it has recently been "falsified." His view is like that of the Gnostics we have mentioned, although their notion was that the true and authentic doctrine had somehow been corrupted at a very early date and that they were simply recovering it. There is every reason to suppose that neither view is acceptable, although the more orthodox idea is closer to the truth. Neither side recognized that what later came to be called heresy was potentially present from the beginning (as was orthodoxy), and that to some extent heresy was outmoded orthodoxy. Neither side was really interested in history.

In the light of these discussions, it is quite remarkable to find that Origen, at the beginning of his treatise *De principiis*, insisted that the apostles had set forth the essentials of the faith in their preaching (largely as transmitted in the New Testament) but had usually not discussed the rational proof of their assertions. Some articles of faith were simply stated (*quia sint*) without analysis of circumstances (*quomodo sint*) or origins (*unde sint*).[14] Among the questions which the apostles thus left open for future discussion were the following:

(1) whether the Holy Spirit was generated or not;[15]
(2) whether the soul was transmitted in human semen (either as *ratio* or as substance) or had some other origin; whether this origin was generated or not; whether the soul came from outside the body or not;[16]
(3) what the devil and his angels are and how they exist (many hold that the devil was an apostate

---

[14] Origen, *De principiis*, 1 praef. 3 (p. 9, 4–8 Koetschau).
[15] *Ibid.*, praef. 4 (p. 11, 4–5).   [16] *Ibid.*, praef. 5 (p. 13, 7–11).

angel who persuaded many other angels to fall with him);[17]

(4) what existed before the creation of this world and what will exist after it;[18]

(5) whether or not the philosophical term "incorporeal" is found in scripture under another guise, and whether or not God is corporeal or incorporeal (the same question must be raised in relation to Christ, the Holy Spirit, the soul, and every rational being);[19]

(6) the time when angels were created, as well as details about them;[20]

(7) whether the sun, the moon, and the stars are animate or not.[21]

If one takes all these questions together, it is obvious that they are concerned with the basic question as to what kind of philosophical-theological framework is to be provided for the apostolic preaching. Indeed, since the fifth point involves the incorporeality of God, Christ, and the Holy Spirit, it is clear that for Origen the range of unanswered theological problems was very wide indeed, though we must admit at once that he was fairly sure that he could answer them. The basic distinction he makes (*quia* versus *quomodo* and *unde*) is the conventional Hellenistic distinction between existence (what the apostles discussed) and essence (what they did not).[22]

---

[17] *Ibid.*, praef. 6 (p. 13, 12–17). [18] *Ibid.*, praef. 7 (p. 14, 1–5).
[19] *Ibid.*, praef. 9 (p. 15, 20–27). [20] *Ibid.*, praef. 10 (p. 16, 1–3).
[21] *Ibid.* (p. 16, 7–8).
[22] Cf. A.-J. Festugière, *La révélation d'Hermès Trismégiste, IV* (Paris, 1954), 6–17.

Bibliography

I GENERAL
BIBLIOGRAPHY

A. CHRISTIAN AND GNOSTIC WRITINGS: TEXTS AND INDEXES

1. THE APOSTOLIC FATHERS

Texts

F. X. Funk, K. Bihlmeyer, and W. Schneemelcher. Die Apostolischen Väter, Vol. I. Tübingen, 1956.
M. Whittaker. Der Hirt des Hermas. Berlin, 1956.

Index and Lexicon

E. J. Goodspeed. Index Patristicus. Leipzig, 1907 (reprinted, Naperville, Ill., 1960).
W. Bauer, W. F. Arndt, and F. W. Gingrich. A Greek-English Lexicon of the New Testament and Other Early Christain Literature. Chicago, 1957.

2. THE GREEK APOLOGISTS

Texts

J. C. T. Otto. Corpus Apologetarum Christianorum Saeculi Secundi. 9 vols. Jena, 1851–81.
E. J. Goodspeed. Die ältesten Apologeten. Göttingen, 1914.
C. Bonner. The Homily on the Passion by Melito Bishop of Sardis. London, 1940.
B. Lohse. Die Passa-Homilie des Bischofs Meliton von Sardes. Leiden, 1958.
M. Testuz. Papyrus Bodmer XIII: Méliton de Sardes, Homélie sur la Pâque. Coligny-Geneva, 1960.
E. Schwartz. Tatiani Oratio ad Graecos. (Texte und Untersuchungen 4, 1.) Leipzig, 1888.

Index

E. J. Goodspeed. Index Apologeticus. Leipzig, 1912.

3. IRENAEUS

Texts

W. W. Harvey. Sancti Irenaei Episcopi Lugdunensis Libri quinque adversus haereses. 2 vols. Cambridge, 1857.
A. Rousseau, B. Hemmerdinger, L. Doutreleau, and C. Mercier. Irénée de Lyon: Contre les hérésies, Livre IV. Paris, 1965.

Index

B. Reynders. Lexique comparé du texte grec et des versions . . . de l' "Adversus haereses" de saint Irénée. 2 vols. Louvain, 1954.

4. CLEMENT OF ALEXANDRIA

O. Stählin. Clemens Alexandrinus: Werke. 4 vols. Berlin, 1905–36.
R. P. Casey. The Excerpta ex Theodoto of Clement of Alexandria. London, 1935.
F. M. Sagnard. Clément d'Alexandrie: Extraits de Théodote. Paris, 1948.

5. HIPPOLYTUS

P. Wendland. Hippolytus: Refutatio omnium haeresium. Berlin, 1916.

6. ORIGEN

E. Klostermann et. al. Origenes: Werke. 12 vols. to date. Berlin, 1899–.
J. Scherer. Entretien d'Origène avec Héraclide et les évêques ses collègues sur le Père, le Fils, et l'âme. (Publi-

cations de la Société Fouad I de Papyrologie, Textes et Documents, IX.) Cairo, 1949.

7. GNOSTIC DOCUMENTS

W. Till. Die gnostischen Schriften des koptischen Papyrus Berolinensis 8502. (Texte und Untersuchungen 60.) Berlin, 1955.

M. Krause and P. Labib. Die drei Versionen des Apokryphon des Johannes im Koptischen Museum zu Alt-Kairo. Wiesbaden, 1962.

S. Giversen. Apocryphon Johannis. Copenhagen, 1963.

B. BACKGROUND: TEXTS AND STUDIES

Albinus. Text in C. F. Hermann, Platonis Dialogi, VI (Leipzig, 1880), 152–89.

H. von Arnim. Stoicorum veterum fragmenta. 4 vols. Leipzig, 1905–24.

R. Beutler. "Numenios," in A. Pauly and G. Wissowa, Realencyclopädie der classischen Altertumswissenschaft, Supplementband VII (Stuttgart, 1940), 664–78.

H. Chadwick. Early Christian Thought and the Classical Tradition. Oxford, 1966.

J. Daniélou. Théologie du judéo-christianisme. Tournai, 1958.

J. Daniélou. Message évangélique et culture hellénistique. Tournai, 1961.

H. Diels. Doxographi Graeci. Berlin, 1879 (reprinted 1929).

E. R. Dodds. Pagan and Christian in an Age of Anxiety. Cambridge, 1965.

R. M. Grant. The Letter and the Spirit. London, 1957.

R. M. Grant. "Scripture, Rhetoric and Theology in Theophilus," in Vigiliae Christianae 13 (1959), 33–45.

R. M. Grant. Gnosticism and Early Christianity. New York, 1959. (Revised, La gnose et les origines chrétiennes. Paris, 1964.)

R. M. Grant. "Early Christianity and Pre-Socratic Philosophy," in Wolfson Jubilee Volumes (Jerusalem, 1965), 357–84.

R. P. C. Hanson. Tradition in the Early Church. London, 1962.

E. Hatch. The Influence of Greek Ideas on Christianity. New ed. by F. C. Grant. New York, 1957.

W. Jaeger. The Theology of the Early Greek Philosophers. Oxford, 1947.

E.-A. Leemans. Studie over den Wijsgeer Numenius van Apamea met Uitgave der Fragmenten. Brussels, 1937.

A. D. Nock. Conversion. Oxford, 1933.

A. D. Nock. Early Gentile Christianity. New ed. New York, 1964.

W. Theiler. Die Vorbereitung des Neuplatonismus. Berlin, 1930.

J. H. Waszink. "Bemerkungen zum Einfluss des Platonismus im frühen Christentum," in Vigiliae Christianae 19 (1965), 129–62.

R. E. Witt. Albinus and the History of Middle Platonism. Cambridge, 1937.

H. A. Wolfson. Philo. 2 vols. Cambridge, Mass., 1947.

H. A. Wolfson. The Philosophy of the Church Fathers. Vol. I. Cambridge, Mass., 1956.

II GOD THE FATHER

A. W. Argyle. God in the New Testament. London, 1965.

M. Elze. Tatian und seine Theologie. Göttingen, 1960.

S. Esh. "Der Heilige (er sei gepriesen)." Zur Geschichte einer nach-biblisch-hebräischen Gottesbezeichnung. Leiden, 1957.

A.-J. Festugière. La révélation d'Hermès Trismégiste. Vol. IV: Le Dieu inconnu et la gnose. Paris, 1954.

B. Gaertner. The Areopagus Speech and Natural Revelation. Uppsala, 1955.

E. R. Goodenough. The Theology of Justin Martyr. Jena, 1923.

H. Hommel. Schöpfer und Erhalter. Berlin, 1956.

K. E. Kirk. The Vision of God. London, 1932.

J. Kroll. Die Lehren des Hermes Trismegistos. Münster, 1928.

A. Marmorstein. The Old Rabbinic Doctrine of God. Vol. I. London, 1927.

E. Norden. Agnostos Theos. Leipzig, 1913.

R. A. Norris, Jr. God and World in Early Christian Theology. New York, 1965.

A. Nygren. Agape and Eros (rev. translation). London, 1953.

E. F. Osborn. The Philosophy of Clement of Alexandria. Cambridge, 1957.

W. Pannenberg. "Die Aufnahme des philosophischen Gottesbegriffs als dogmatisches Problem der frühchristlichen Theologie," Zeitschrift für Kirchengeschichte 70 (1959), 1–45.

E. Peterson. ΕΙΣ ΘΕΟΣ. Göttingen, 1926.

M. Pohlenz. Vom Zorne Gottes. Göttingen, 1909.

G. L. Prestige. God in Patristic Thought. London, 1936.

C. M. Walsh. The Doctrine of Creation. London, 1910.

III THE SON OF GOD

W. Bousset. Kyrios Christos. Göttingen, 1913.

O. Cullmann. The Christology of the New Testament. Philadelphia, 1959.

F. Hahn. Christologische Hoheitstitel: Ihre Geschichte im frühen Christentum. Göttingen, 1963.

A. Houssiau. La christologie de saint Irénée. Louvain, 1955.

V. A. S. Little. The Christology of the Apologists. New York, 1935.

A. E. J. Rawlinson. The New Testament Doctrine of the Christ. London, 1926.

IV THE HOLY SPIRIT AND THE TRINTY

C. K. Barrett. The Holy Spirit and the Gospel Tradition. New York, 1947.

P. Gerlitz. Ausserchristliche Einflüsse auf die Entwicklung des christlichen Trinitätsdogmas. Leiden, 1963.

J. N. D. Kelly. Early Christian Doctrines. New York, 1958. pp. 83–108.

G. Kretschmar. Studien zur frühchristlichen Trinitätstheologie. Tübingen, 1956.

J. Lebreton. Histoire du dogme de la Trinité des origines au Concile de Nicée. 2 vols. Paris, 1927–28.

H. R. Niebuhr. "The Doctrine of the Trinity and the Unity of the Church," Theology Today 3 (1946–47), 371–84.

T. Rüsch. Die Entstehung der Lehre vom Heiligen Geist. Zurich, 1952.

G. Verbeke. L'évolution de la doctrine de la Pneuma. Louvain, 1945.

Indexes

BIBLICAL PASSAGES

ANCIENT WRITERS AND WRITINGS

MODERN WRITERS

THE EARLY CHRISTIAN DOCTRINE OF GOD

was composed, printed, and bound by
Kingsport Press, Inc., Kingsport, Tennessee.
The type is Janson, and the
paper is Warren's Olde Style.
Design is by Edward G. Foss.

DATE DUE

DEMCO, INC. 38-2931